Tolstoi

World University Library

The World University Library is an international series
of books, each of which has been specially commissioned.
The authors are leading scientists and scholars from all over
the world who, in an age of increasing specialization, see the
need for a broad, up-to-date presentation of their subject.
The aim is to provide authoritative introductory books for
students which will be of interest also to the general
reader. Publication of the series takes place in Britain,
France, Germany, Holland, Italy, Spain, Sweden and
the United States.

Frontispiece A contrast of styles in Algeria.

Evelyne Sullerot

Woman, Society
and Change

Translated from the French
by Margaret Scotford Archer

396.9
Su5w

World University Library

McGraw-Hill Book Company
New York Toronto

Photoset by BAS Printers Limited, Wallop, Hampshire, England
Manufactured by LIBREX, Italy

1592713

Contents

Who in the world would dare to write a book about man – simply as a representative of the male sex? The question would at once be asked: 'What man?' One from an industrialised country, or from a backward part of the world? A young man, a grown-up, an elderly person? Intellectual or farmer? And above all, how and on what assumption would the material be handled? Why, indeed, make such an assessment? Modern man in relation to what norms? The subject would necessarily become a treatment of contemporary society, with modern man compared to his recent or historical predecessor.

But when woman is concerned, the subject loses its daring and becomes more precise. Although there are apparently few features in common between a woman of Upper Volta and a woman of New York, between a teenager and a woman of seventy, between the mother of a large family and a single woman, between a farmer's wife and a career woman, an attempt to describe over half of the human race, despite its diversity, does not strike one as absurd. This is due to a single reason, be it good or bad in itself, and that is that this half of humanity can be studied in relation to the other half, but this does not work the other way round.

Indeed it is only by reference to man's position in each society, country, social class, environment, age group or occupation, that one can speak of the position of women. One is not just describing but actually comparing, as it is the sum of differences between the status of men and of women which leads one to the idea that women have a distinctive position in society. In itself, this does not simplify the task very much, since before being able to speak of *woman* one must take account of the huge variety in the way of life of people whose only common feature is their sex. However, a catalogue of these different modes of life would not be very meaningful unless comparisons were made with those of their male partners.

At birth, every woman is endowed with sexual characteristics finding expression in her erotic and reproductive roles which are

8

The followers of the socialist Comte de
Saint Simon set up a communistic society
during the year 1832. The women were
given complete equality even, as shown here
to the extent of doing the men's work.

quite different from those of man. Moreover, she must adopt social attitudes that clearly define her as a woman: certain roles and certain social characteristics, of which most have no apparent relationship with woman's special physiology. Thus, in no country or society do women dress like men. Often the very language is different, for example, the female Californian Indians used to speak a special dialect in which almost every word was different from that used by the men. Many languages – Japanese is one example – still contain significant differences between male and female word endings. To a lesser extent the same is true for languages of Greco-Latin or Semitic origin in which adjectives and past participles have different endings when they refer to men or women.

Usually from childhood upwards women are given special tasks and duties. All these characteristics add up to a kind of *social sex* which defines woman's place in society just as much as does her biological sex. Following Margaret Mead, it is interesting to note that these characteristics, roles and attitudes which make up the social sex are not uniform in every culture. While, in the same animal species, all the males and all the females behave in the same way and take on the same roles in mating, in nest building, in rearing the young, in displaying the appropriate plumage or coat, the social symbols of femininity and female roles vary significantly from one human society to another. In one society, women do not work in the fields; in another, they are responsible for all agricultural labour. In one, the father dictates the education of his children; in the other, the wife has a near-monopoly over bringing them up. In one, trousers are an exclusively masculine garb; in another, feminine. Any inversion of those roles or characteristics creates a sense of scandal and an impression that the world is upside down. Indeed, it was under the general title 'The world upside down' that popular prints depicting social customs but reversing sexual roles were published in Flanders in the seventeenth and eighteenth centuries. Yet ethnology makes it clear that these conventions are relative to each society and that what is 'the right way round' for some, is 'upside down' for others. It was early

10

A Rwanda woman washing her crop of yams. African men usually do the heavy work of ploughing, but thereafter the women are expected to take charge of the day-to-day routine of food production.

noted by Strabo of the Germanic tribes that they divided tasks between men and women in a way which was 'quite the reverse of ours'.

Nevertheless, no society has so far avoided these distinctions, even though the interchangeability of male and female roles is ample proof of how artificial such distinctions are.

Differentiation and change

Yet these distinctions, rigid in primitive and traditional societies, are more fluid in modern, rapidly changing ones. In the latter, they are being increasingly challenged, generally by women themselves, who feel that such discrimination is not to their advantage. However, the division between the sexes is everywhere maintained. It is almost as if humanity wanted for ever to put off the time when the sexes would not be socially differentiated – a situation often wrongly confused with the sexless society.

Moreover, social change brought about by technical development, industrialisation, urbanisation and political upheavals always seems more rapid for men than for women. Thus, in traditional societies, the position of women is still fairly well delineated by the continued role division between the sexes. But, in modern societies, it is the time-lag between social change for men and for women which is the main index of role differentiation and consequently of the position of women in relation to men. For example, it is not very significant to note that in the United States almost all women have a driving licence and drive cars just like men, while elsewhere cars are driven mainly by men. It is only when motoring is universal and the ability to drive is commonplace, without prestige and relatively boring, that all women get a chance to do it. When cars were scarce and represented prestige and power, women were seldom allowed to own and use them. The same time-lag is found in access to the professions as they were founded one after the other during the process of industrialisation. It is found also in the exercise of civil rights and in the level of

Rifle drill for girls at a technical
academy in Peking. Communism has radically
changed the traditional role of women.

13

educational attainment. A study of statistics on illiteracy shows
that in the vast majority of countries it is mainly to be found
among women. However, in countries which are completely
literate, it is at the level of secondary, technical and above all
higher education that the time-lag is most evident between the
mass of men and of women. It is not typically masculine to be
able to read and typically feminine not to; it is not typically
masculine to have a doctorate and typically feminine not to. What
is more important than the performance of women in one country
or another is either that this time-lag continues to exist between
progress for men and for women, or that the gap is being closed.

Our societies are evolving further and further away from cultural
patterns where tasks were distributed in a way which had some
physiological justification, for example, in terms of the relative
physical strength of men and women. Automation and other
technical advances have increasingly done away with these logical
justifications which used to be considered natural laws. The basis
on which tasks, roles and rights are allotted to each sex and the
justification of differences between them needs to be re-examined
in modern society. The ways in which such differences are maintained, the degree to which they are accepted and the grounds on
which they are challenged or attacked call for investigation.

It is clear that women are dissatisfied almost throughout the
world and that a constant debate about their position is in progress. Almost every constitution proclaims equality of rights and
responsibilities for citizens of both sexes. In practice the resistance
to legal equality is remarkably strong, particularly as it comes from
women as often as from men. The underlying reason is that the
position of women has always or nearly always been defined in
terms of their *role*. Women have always been given a specific role,
mainly in the family, and their social role has evolved from it.
Incidentally, it is significant to note that one has had to wait until
the second half of the twentieth century for a debate about the
father's role. It was initiated in Sweden, where it was pursued with
the same intensity as debates about mothers, and relied on those

arguments usually reserved for discussing the maternal role. As soon as the functions of women were no longer narrowly linked to physiological factors and ceased to be shaped exclusively by demographic and economic imperatives, a search for moral justification started. The role of women developed a 'sacred' character and any modification in it triggered off an ideological debate, so that at present all discussion of their position has moral and ideological overtones.

To a certain extent the present condition of women could be compared with that of developing countries in relation to the developed ones. The efforts to reduce the gap between rich and poor countries could be taken as a guide in creating equality between men and women. Nevertheless, such an analogy would fail to take account of the interconnexions between moral prejudice and preconceived ideas and the economic and legal issues which are inseparable from 'the problem of women'.

An understanding of the present situation would not be complete without a knowledge, albeit slight, of the past. Certainly the emphasis should be on recent causes bringing about modifications in the position of modern women, and principally on demographic and economic causes. Even so we are still the heirs of antiquated notions which influence our thinking, and it would be wise to bear them in mind.

Resistance to change

From the beginning of the nineteenth century, certain writers became interested in this fundamental problem of woman's position. Thus Gustav Geiger, the Swedish sociologist, wrote, 'The position of women in a society provides an exact measure of the development of that society'. The French utopian philosopher Charles Fourier made a similar statement in 1805, but went even further in postulating a 'general principle' that 'social progress and changing eras are linked to increases in women's freedom, and social decadence is accompanied by a decrease in their freedom'.

By 'changing eras' is meant what we would now call 'social change' or mutation. According to Fourier, the study of woman's position would be vital because it would indicate the trend of social change as a whole.

Social change is usually synonymous with changes in social structure. It is clear that the position of women represents a coherent structure in which all the elements are integrated: ideology, role in the family, role in society, economic role, sphere of activity and sphere of forbidden activity, etc. These components of the female position are closely intercorrelated. It would be interesting to know whether a change in one of these components would automatically change the whole structure. Only a brief review of the past can provide support for this hypothesis.

An historical review would still be necessary even if the theory of structure did not prove valid, in order to construct a more evolutionary theory, or simply to abandon both theories and recognise the complexity and originality of the problem of woman's condition.

Everywhere one hears of change in the situation of modern women, of the 'undermining of traditional values', usually with fears about the emergence of a new breed of women. There is no need to go further than the national press or women's magazines to become aware of this. At the same time it should be remembered that there is nothing new about these statements, as a glance at such magazines published over the last two hundred years shows. They are full either of laments or praise of women's development and the corresponding revolution in traditional customs. Every three months the same points of view are aired anew in our modern press: the position of women is changing so rapidly that the future of the world is endangered and moral standards may be threatened. All statements about progress in woman's lot are fraught with concern about the potential disruption of society. Even while such articles hypocritically applaud the advances made by women, and over-emphasise it at will, it is easy to perceive that they seek to instil fear of change, to magnify the eternal nature of

eminine duties and to see it as the cornerstone of social stability. This choir singing in unison about the dire consequences of emancipation should be mistrusted. A content analysis of countless articles on woman's position over more than two and a half centuries yields curious results. It appears that throughout this period all changes were always resented as disastrous for morality. Grandmothers and great-grandmothers were virtuous, modern women are no longer so. (This was written in 1750 and in 1850 in almost exactly the same terms as it is today.) The belief lurks among men that the female golden age is firmly located in the past and that only prehistoric wives were perfectly moral and perfectly dutiful in accepting their 'natural' station in life.

This great fear of women's emancipation has led to so many false interpretations of alleged change that extreme care is now essential. Only the study of the past can provide an exact assessment of this evolution. It can show whether women's status improved as a result of their own efforts or whether it merely reflected changes in society brought about by men, whether women have always followed or have been innovators. If they have only been followers throughout history, it is hardly worthwhile to outline their present position in contemporary society. But it does seem that a radical change has occurred in the modern world and that we are now standing on the brink of a profound transformation. How it will take place, which particular adjustment will trigger off a chain reaction throughout the whole structure, how it will affect society at large and the opposite sex – these are questions which can only be answered through the study of history and the replacement of myth by knowledge.

1 The patriarchal system

Three main traditions have held sway in Europe and have eventually merged: the Greco-Latin system, the Judaic and the Scandinavian-German patterns. The latter prevailed in the north and the west of Europe before and during the Roman conquest, and spread during Rome's decline. It was Christianity which modified and unified these three social systems. On the other hand, the Confucian, Hindu and later the Islamic traditions held sway over the East with hardly any contact with the West until the nineteenth century. This extremely simplified picture should not lead us to forget that none of these patterns remained stable over time. For example, considerable change in family life occurred between Peloponnesian Greece and pre-Christian Rome. It would be too much of a generalisation to state that the position of women improves with the development of civilisations; sometimes the opposite appears to be the case. As a rule it is in the early periods of each civilisation that the least difference exists between the position of men and that of women. As a civilisation asserts and refines itself, the gap between the relative status of men and women widens (in spite of Charles Fourier's feminist statement quoted on page 14 – although his use of the terms 'social progress' and 'social decadence' may have been misunderstood).

While Prometheus had to steal fire from the gods to make himself their equal, Woman – who alone can give life – had no need of the Promethean fire. But did her fecundity give her power, did it confer on her a supremacy in ancient societies? Did a true matriarchy really precede patriarchy as a system of family organisation? Many have been the theories about the primitive matriarchy, many are the traces left behind by matrilineal societies in Africa, Melanesia and South America, and many also have been the myths and legends, at times corroborated by archaeological discoveries, of the rule of women in ancient civilisations. It is uncertain whether these legends describe reality or whether they have merely become exaggerated and distorted in the process of telling. It is difficult to interpret the legend of the Amazons, or that of the Chinese kingdom known as 'the Country of Women' (where a queen and a minor queen ruled) or finally the Czech legend of the Kingdom of Vlasta, the woman who repelled Charles Martel founded Drewin, the City of Women, and governed Bohemia until it was forcibly recaptured by men. Such stories of female rule are always relegated to the distant past and one may wonder whether they are not used to counterbalance the pattern of patriarchy. However, it is unclear if these legends have been invented after the event to provide a parallel to what exists now and thus to satisfy the tendency of the human mind to think in binary terms by imagining an opposing reign succeeding another. In any case the link which would explain how the rule of men succeeded that of women has always been missing.

Patriarchal rule as a coherent system

Historically the strictest patriarchal pattern has dominated the Greco-Roman, Semitic, Indian, Chinese and Japanese civilisations. In this system, the reproductive function of women has appeared at the same time both as their justification in the world and the reason for their subordination. From this follow all the other features of woman's position and it is interesting to see which elements in this chain, when modified, bring about a change in the whole structure. But while answering this question, an assessment should be made of what remains of this legacy of the past.

Fertility and adultery. Before all else, the wife was considered as a breeding machine to perpetuate the male line of the husband, the tribe and the race. Therefore the punishments for female adultery were extremely severe, as by this act the wife asserted her individuality, her free will, her right to choose. Such an assertion was seen as a threat to the whole male-centred structure. In Judaic society the adulterous wife was stoned; in Greek society, if she was not put to death she became infamous and was forced to dress in a way which would enable others to recognise her transgression; in China and Vietnam she passed through the Seven Hells. Despite hese variations, the husband everywhere had the power of life or death over his adulterous wife. The severity of this condemnation did not arise so much from emotional jealousy as from the fact that the preservation of the system required the wife to fulfil her reproductive role in accordance with strict rules. If she were to assert her individuality by committing adultery, she would destroy the fabric of the system, and the family name, property, titles, power, nationality and other prerogatives would no longer be transmitted by the male line.

Love as a sentiment is so lacking in this system that the wife was bequeathed or lent in order to perpetuate the race. Thus in Greece, Israel and India, the widow was part of the husband's estate and was left to his eldest male relative like a chattel. The barren wife was sometimes approached by the brother of her husband, with his consent, so that the future of the line could be guaranteed. The rules of repudiation were related to this overriding goal. Thus, according to the Manu Code of India, if a wife had no children, she could be banished after eight years; if all her children were dead, she could be dismissed after ten years; if she had nothing but girls, she could be repudiated after the eleventh year. Modern science in fact shows that it is the odd chromosome in the male semen which determines the sex of the child, so that the mother does not influence it. Yet thousands of women have been repudiated for this reason, at the time when the patriarchal system was alleged to embody the natural order.

According to Mosaic law, the Israelite had the right to repudiate his infertile wife and to father children with his servant. The legitimate wife, if kept in the conjugal home, would help and aid the servant in her delivery. The story of Abraham and Sarah illustrates this practice. In Greece, the man – even though he had only one legitimate wife – could nevertheless surround himself by a swarm of slave mistresses and have children by them. In the East, the present practice of polygamy witnesses the same idea of the wife as a breeding machine placed at the service of the male, his group, family, tribe and people. In the old Germanic tribes, the adulterous

wife was also put to death or mutilated, and a widow, when she did not commit suicide on the death of her husband – a practice which also occurred in India – was given to her brother-in-law. This kind of ritual suicide did not reflect private grief or desperation, but expressed obedience to social constraints.

Thus the system might be monogamous or polygamous, but this made little difference to the overall patriarchal society.

Domestic confinement. A direct consequence of the system described above was the desire to confine women in the home, to restrict their movements and to prevent them showing themselves outside. These customs have determined women's activities for centuries and may account for the presence of many acquired characteristics, now considered as innate. The wives were strictly

The gynaeceum, or women's quarters, from an Attic vase painting. Virtuous women were kept safely shut away indoors.

confined to their quarters in Greece, whereas the courtesans, whose job was to give pleasure to man and not to produce his children, were free. Woman was confined indoors, turned into a recluse and often hidden, like the Chinese behind screens and the Moslem behind veils, while man alone had the freedom of the outside world. Socrates claimed that it was thus that the gods had decreed. But this territorial division quickly became a moral one – 'the house is for the good woman, the street for the wicked one' said Menander, repeating a popular cliché. Consequently activities within the house are feminine, those which take place outside – business, politics, war – are masculine. This polarity of inside-outside, *interior-exterior*, imperceptibly became a distinction between *inferiority-superiority*. Gradually activities conducted inside were considered inferior to those performed outside. Female tasks,

Greek hetaerae were able to mix freely
with men. A 'free woman' was for a
long time considered a 'loose woman'.

just as necessary in life as those accomplished outside, soon became despised. The spatial division between the man and the woman is not an unavoidable consequence of their physiological differences, but only an important element of the patriarchal system whose legacy endures in our own civilisation.

Property. A third and related characteristic of the system is that women were excluded from owning and disposing of property. The Manu Code of India specified that everything acquired either by the wife or the slave belonged to the husband or the master. In Greece, the wife could never dispose of her property. She passed from the tutelage of her father to that of her husband, or of his male relative on widowhood, or finally of her own son if he was the only man left in the family. She could be given a dowry, but this would not become her property. Such was not the case in Sparta or in early Rome, where barbarian family customs still prevailed. But when Rome became prosperous a patriarchal system was enforced, and attempts were made to limit women's right of possession. The Oppian law, which sought to restrict women's ownership of clothing and jewellery, caused a female rebellion and had to be abrogated. Shortly afterwards Cato supported the adoption of a law forbidding women to inherit more than 100,000 sesterces. Again, the Jewish tradition excluded the daughter from her father's estate, unless he had no sons. In that case she had to marry a member of her own tribe and credit him with the money, land or property that she had inherited. Moreover, the Jewess was not considered a legitimate wife but a concubine unless she brought property to the marriage, nor did she have any control over her portion.

Civic rights. The fourth link in this chain was that women had no civic role. In Greece they had no more public rights than slaves, minors or foreigners. Solon regulated even their right to travel. Within the city they could not even cross the streets unless they were in a carriage preceded by a torch-bearer. The only right they were granted was that of defending themselves in court or being witnesses in trials. Even this prerogative became more and more restricted and was finally withdrawn in Rome by Justinian. In the predominantly religious Jewish community, this deprivation of civic rights extended to the majority of religious observances, from which women were excluded. However, Greek and Roman women joined in many religious celebrations and had specific roles to play in the religious life of their community. Their creeds and mythologies were not uniformly hostile to women nor derogatory about the female character. On the other hand, Judaism, accusing woman of the original sin, reduced her to something impure and untrustworthy, responsible for the fall of man. Hence she is forbidden to touch the Book of Laws, excluded from religious learning in the temple and, in this respect, treated like a male slave. The temple ceremonies can only be celebrated by men and for men, since ten male witnesses must be present, regardless of the number of women. Giving birth to a son leaves the wife impure for a week, giving birth to a daughter leaves her impure for two. The woman is sullied and she contaminates. 'Blessed be Thou, O God, who did not make me a woman!' exclaims man.

Islam too makes use of this notion of impurity and uncleanliness to exclude women from the city and from religion, where they are nothing more than subdued onlookers. Oriental religions are even more emphatic in their denunciation of female uncleanliness. In China during the early historical period it was the custom for the family to take on mourning when a daughter was born. The girl was placed on the ground next to bricks and tiles, which represented 'symbols of abjection and the evils which were to accompany her throughout her life'! Pan Hoei Pan explains, tiles were used because they were exposed to damage from above and bricks because they were meant to be crushed under foot. To kill a daughter was not classed as a crime and girl children were often left to die from exposure or were simply sold. Pan Hoei Pan wrote in *Seven Articles Intended for Women*, a book which appeared in the first century AD: 'Never let us forget that we belong to the lowest form of human life. We must expect only contempt. There will never be disillusionment for a woman so long as she remembers that she will always be made to suffer by those with whom she lives.'

Changes due to Christianity

To sum up, both ancient philosophies and ancient religions dictated the same social position for women. While the Greeks and the Romans excluded women because they despised their abilities, which were mocked by Aristophanes and Plautus, the Jewish, Muslim and Oriental religions debarred them because of their innate uncleanliness. Hence the former denied them secular rights in the city, while the latter considered them as contaminating all they touched. A parallel approach thus prevailed in both ideologies.

Christianity was to break this chain of reasoning. It constituted a new charter of freedom for women, since it gave hope to all the oppressed, the humble and the condemned. 'Before God there is neither slave nor master, neither Jew nor Greek, neither woman nor man.' She is exempted from her inborn uncleanliness. Christ touched the untouchable woman and forgave Mary Magdalene. He did not differentiate between male and female sinners. Rehabilitated as a person and relieved of her uncleanliness, the Greek, Jewish, Roman and Barbarian woman who embraced the Christian faith smashed the structure which imprisoned her. Indeed there were many women among the first Christians and they proved active in the early Church.

The idea of equality before God which replaced that of inferiority and impurity in the patriarchal system seemed likely to destroy the whole ancient edifice and to herald a revolution for women.

But, on the contrary, the old system gave way very little and recovered ground very quickly. Theologians can discuss for ever whether Saint Paul, when he claimed that woman had committed the original sin, that it is good for man to have no contact with her, and that women should be obedient and silent, was continuing the teachings of Christ, expressing his personal views, or even expressing leanings obvious to a psychoanalyst. This is of little importance. What is significant is that although one major ideological obstacle to female emancipation had been removed, the rest did not follow. Very quickly women came to represent 'the gates of hell' to the Church, and the Council of Metz recommended that the priests should avoid their mothers and sisters. Unclean once more, women remained of no consequence. At the Council of Macon women were granted a soul by a majority of only one vote. To Thomas Aquinas, woman was but an accidental being. Much later still, Luther reiterated the right of the husband to repudiate his wife if she resisted him and to take her servant instead. The Protestants at the Wittenberg Conference even tried to prove that women were not human beings.

Paradoxically it was through exaggerating the 'sin' of woman and introducing the cult of virginity that Christianity slowly loosened the hold of the traditional system. Celebrated nuns, saints and teachers, women like Hildegarde of Brockelheim, Bridget of Sweden, Teresa of Avila and the Abbesses of Fontevrault, demonstrated through their knowledge, authority and spiritual flame the falsity of the Roman accusation: 'Tota mulier in utero'. But these were virgins, not ordinary women, and their exceptional lives did not change the overall judgment. To accept the dangers of childbirth remained the common duty of women. As the encyclical *Humanae Vitae* clearly shows, Catholic philosophy has not accepted the right of women to freely decide when or whether to have children. Furthermore, women have always been excluded from the ministry and it is only in recent years that a few have been allowed to take orders in some Protestant denominations.

Economic factors

Can it be that economic factors rather than ideology govern our understanding of the position of woman?

It may be indicative that there were fewer differences between

the status of women and of men in Germany, Scandinavia and
Gaul at these periods. Referring back to the four previous types of
restriction imposed on women, we note that:
1 Adulterous women were strictly punished, but men too were
discouraged from committing adultery. Monogamy was not interpreted as applying to one sex only and therefore there were fewer
differences between men and women in this respect.
2 The woman was no recluse: her childhood was spent like that
of boys. 'There is no hothouse for young women', wrote Tacitus,
astounded by the strength and height of Germanic women. In
Finland, women hunted with men, and in Germany accompanied
them to war. They travelled with men, their faces unveiled.
3 In Germany, it was the husband who brought the dowry to his
wife, and this was not a symbolic gift, but consisted of horses,
cattle and weapons. It was the women who raised animals and
undertook the agricultural work. The *eddas* of twelfth-century
Scandinavia tell of the active role played by women and the rights
they enjoyed. Not only could they inherit, but they were also the

The eighteenth century strongly idealised the role of
the mother, satirised here in the engraving by Massart,
after the painting 'La Mère bien-aimée' by Greuze.

33

sole guardians of books, as though this were an acknowledgment
of their intelligence.
4 Women played an active role in religion and, at least in Britain
and Gaul, were admitted to religious offices like men. They were
also active in the administration of their tribes, being found here
and there as councillors and even as civilian and military judges.
It was the women of Gaul who settled the disputes between the
local tribes and Hannibal's troops when he crossed Aquitaine.
They shared fully in the decision-making of their tribe or of their
community.

The economic roles of women in patriarchal and barbaric systems are approximately comparable. In both cases they were as
productive as men or more so. In these primitive economies relying
on handicrafts, most artifacts were produced by women. The
whole process of manufacturing textiles, from the shearing of
sheep or the cultivation and retting of hemp to the sewing of
clothes, including spinning and weaving, was accomplished by
female labour. Women were responsible also for almost every
stage of food cultivation and preparation: they alone drew water,
they grew and picked vegetables, cereals and fruit, they gathered
olives, they raised poultry, they milled flour (operating the stone
mills), they baked bread, cooked meals, cured meat, and so on.
The peoples of Germany, Scandinavia, Brittany or Gaul did not
practise slavery and in consequence left a greater amount of the
productive processes to their women. However, work was rewarded
with respect, whereas the Greeks, for example, despised both
their women and their slaves, since both were condemned to 'work'
instead of 'thinking' or 'enjoying life'.

The main difference appears to be derived from the type of
property holding which led by its very nature to an urban rather
than a rural economy. The Greco-Roman, Judaic and Oriental
worlds were based on private property. The peoples of north and
west Europe had to a much greater extent – despite local variations
– collective property holdings. The former rapidly became urbanised and settled in centres of commerce, whereas the latter led a

semi-nomadic life and operated a barter economy.

The expansion of the Roman Empire rapidly spread the idea and the practice that private property was reserved for men under Roman law (in particular by the *jura privata, jus commercii* and *jus conubii*). To Hegel, the outstanding characteristic of Rome was the plebeian-patrician division. It could be argued that this included a division between men and women: a distinction between those who owned and those who were propertyless, those who exercised rights and those who enjoyed none. Gradually Roman law prevailed in north and west Europe and women, having lost their property, watched their influence shrink. Whereas collectivism had integrated them into the community, the reign of private ownership and the beginnings of early capitalism after the end of the Middle Ages gradually increased the distance between the position of men and women. Clearly the way of life of Germanic women, always at work and enduring the hardships of war, appears less enviable than that of the Roman citizeness or that of the woman who belonged to the post-Renaissance bourgeoisie. A similar statement could be made about Soviet women between 1920 and 1960 approximately, or Chinese women in the popular communes, whose lot would appear to most western women much harder than their own. However, the distance dividing men from women is much less in a collectivist system than under capitalism. In all capitalist economies, there is a difference in power, wages, incomes, civic responsibilities, to the disadvantage of women, who are turned into a female *Lumpenproletariat* occupying the lowest rung of the social ladder. The position of women is altered by economic development – this is obvious when one compares their status in the same society before and after changes in the economic system. It will be shown later that this is particularly striking nowadays with regard to sex distinctions in wage-earning. The transformation is obvious when one studies the transition from medieval society, still impregnated with pre-Roman traditional laws and still relatively collectivist, to the proto-capitalist economy of the Renaissance period with its stress on individual initiative. Detailed

1592713

research over several centuries has established the respective wage scales of men and women employed in agriculture. In the twelfth century, the female wage was approximately eighty per cent of male remuneration, by the end of the fourteenth century, it had shrunk to seventy-five per cent, and in the fifteenth century it was no more than half. In the sixteenth century, despite the growth of humanism, the increased affluence, the faster circulation of gold and the fact that work was considered valuable in itself rather than a necessary evil, women who did the same job as men received only forty per cent of their wages.

Examples of this kind abound in the nineteenth century, when women's lot was at its worst. They were then paid fifty to sixty per cent less than men for the same work. For example, the male worker in a German paper-mill earned forty-five per cent more than his female counterpart did for producing a thousand sheets of paper. This was just at the time when the speed of industrialisation was giving a new impetus to capitalism.

On the other hand, the Russian Revolution gave the large majority of Russian women the possibility of social integration which they had never experienced before. Similarly, the total economic change brought about in China by the Communist Revolution allowed a quick break from the traditional subordination of women which the uncoordinated attempts of Christian missionaries had failed to secure.

Remains of the patriarchal system

The wife's adultery is no longer punishable by death, but is still considered a more serious offence than the husband's. In Spain and in some parts of Italy, the husband who kills his unfaithful wife is 'avenging his honour' and is either not punished at all or else not severely. This is also the case in many underdeveloped countries, in spite of the egalitarian constitutions they have produced. Throughout the world the position of unmarried mothers may have greatly improved; nevertheless they remain at a serious

36

These prostitutes live in Bombay, in a district known as the cages'. India signed (and in 1953 ratified) the United Nations convention of 1950 which abolished prostitution; but she, like many other countries who also signed the convention, has not been able to implement it.

disadvantage. I am reminded in this connexion of a television programme, recorded in five European countries, which included a sequence about state aid in Sweden for unmarried mothers. Towards the end, it alluded to 'unmarried fathers' who had legally recognised their child when the mother had not done so. Although far less numerous, they were treated like unmarried mothers and granted the same aid. The reaction of viewers in the five countries was characteristic: the mothers had 'sinned' and the assistance they received was only justified by the child's need. But the famous 'unmarried fathers' were heroic and noble. Everyone praised their courage and their unselfishness. Their beautiful gesture was unmarred by any guilt. The sin of the flesh remained a female transgression. A similar prejudice is found in public opinion on the freedom evidenced by English girls in their behaviour and dress, which has been condemned more strongly than any extravagance in male fashions and denounced as a symptom of decadence.

A few years ago I carried out in France a survey on suicide which revealed some interesting attitudes. In the sample, ninety per cent of informants were convinced that Sweden has the highest suicide rate – which is quite untrue. When they were put right and told that the Swiss rate was higher, they made some very revealing comments. It was obvious that Sweden, the antiseptic paradise, was also seen as 'the modernistic nightmare' because girls and women had so much sexual freedom. This freedom, displayed in many commercial films, was bound in their view to result in social disintegration; people in Sweden were bound to commit suicide, to get divorced, to drink heavily and so forth. When they were assured that suicide, homicide and divorce rates were higher in Switzerland than in Sweden, they answered 'And yet the Swiss are such decent people'. They did not admire only the landscape and the institutions, they praised also the quiet and modest behaviour of Swiss women. It was as if women's sexual freedom was considered a major threat to social conservation.

Though adulterous wives are no longer ruthlessly punished, mothers who neglect the upbringing of their children are treated

with growing severity. Since women are no longer required t
devote many years of their life to procreation, they are expected t
take prolonged care of their children instead. This duty is strictl
enforced, in spite of the fact that it is only since the late eighteent
and early nineteenth centuries that the upbringing of childre
after babyhood has been a female responsibility.

Problems resulting from the survival of prostitution

The continued existence of prostitution shows that the old dicho
tomy survives: some women are meant to breed and raise a family
others are intended to give men pleasure. Man is always seen an
recognised as an ambivalent being, torn between freedom an
conformity, between pleasure and morality, between his spiritua
and his animal nature. Each individual is both Jekyll and Hyde
his impulses are diverse and often contradictory. On the othe
hand, it is *womankind*, and not the individual female, who i
considered to be divided in two; wives and mothers are dis
tinguished from goodtime girls, so that both aspects of man'
nature can be satisfied. In most countries each woman must b
either one or the other – and it is almost impossible to pass from th
latter to the former category. It is with difficulty and, in souther
countries, with distaste that the ambivalence of woman's nature i
understood. Thus prostitution is the safest way in which men ca
solve the mathematical problem of sexual life. Only by the existenc
of a group of women who have frequent sexual intercourse wit
various partners can the wives' monogamy and the resulting famil
stability be reconciled with the latent polygamy in which men tak
some pride. To destroy this system would involve the breakup o
the patriarchal tradition and the recognition of sexual freedom fo
both women and men. The Churches have accepted the existenc
of regulated prostitution, although it was not unlike slavery, mor
readily than the idea of sexual freedom for women.

However, the existence of prostitution is less and less acceptabl
in societies which claim to respect the individual. Thus, particularl

since the Second World War, a growing number of countries have abolished or forbidden a regulated prostitution. The United States, the Soviet Union, China, the Scandinavian countries and Pakistan all prohibit it, while England, France, Italy, the Netherlands, Spain, Belgium and Luxemburg are abolitionist. This great step forward has been resisted and often resented as 'immoral', since it implicitly raised the issue of women's sexual freedom. Many countries signed the international convention of 1950 (Convention of the General Assembly of the United Nations abolishing prostitution) without being truly converted to its aims. Thus Germany has a recognised and organised centre of prostitution in Hamburg. Similarly Sydney, Melbourne and Vienna have regulations about a practice officially abolished in both Australia and Austria. Prostitution is also tolerated in many cities, in Marseilles, Rotterdam, Antwerp, even in Paris and Rome, and in various Spanish towns, where old customs survive in spite of inefficient governmental intervention, rather than with the assent of public authorities. Other countries, such as Portugal and Japan, have signed declarations abolishing prostitution, but have not altered their regulations on the subject.

Many other countries legally recognise the need for prostitution and regulate its practice. These include Argentina, Bolivia, Brazil, Mexico, Tunisia, Morocco (where changes have begun, however), Greece and others. It is considered normal that some women will spend a lifetime in this 'trade', kept apart from others and often shut up against their will. Under cover of this 'trade' all kinds of illicit practices go on among those who prey on prostitution and who often constitute an influential political pressure group. Such are the consequences of accepting the old patriarchal approach whereby womankind is divided in two categories. The whole system rests on the economic disadvantage of women. In all countries, most prostitutes are recruited from among girls and women who have been deserted, who have no trade and cannot find a job, rather than from among the pathologically disturbed.

Enduring differences between the sexes

Nowadays property mainly consists in wages and earnings. Whil
in most countries women have gradually acquired the right to ow
goods, to inherit and to dispose of them, they are far from havin
equal access to education, training and jobs or equal remuneratio
for the same work as men. Everywhere, except perhaps in Finlan
and the USSR, the overwhelming majority of underpaid worker
are women. Women are always assumed to be supported by men
and their wages are implicitly or explicitly regarded as an 'addi
tional income'. Hence the economic vulnerability of countles
women living on their own earnings.

It is increasingly infrequent to find women strictly cloistered
Even Moslem countries, the last stronghold of female segregation
are beginning to give up this practice, particularly in the towns
although attempts to eradicate it are slow and unsystematic
However, it is far more important to note that the 'inside/outside
dichotomy is retained in nearly all developed countries, wher
women are not compelled to hide and to stay indoors. Women wh
stay at home are still considered to be morally right, while thos
who go out, even to work, are disapproved of. When someone i
recognised as a career woman, her work should not take her to
far from home. A high-ranking Belgian civil servant told me tha
she was compelled to forego the promotion which was due to her
because a more important post called for more travel and wa
therefore considered unsuitable for a woman, even an unmarrie
one. When I have asked French officials and executives abou
career prospects for women in business, the civil service and th
diplomatic service, I have often been told: 'We shall have to
travel more and more, to be in London one day and in Chicag
or Tokyo the next. This is hardly possible for women.' Similarl
the leaders of large American organisations and of the *Women'*
Bureau assured me that they had difficulties in filling importan
posts, which required frequent visits to Washington, 'since thi
excluded women from the north and the west of the country'

'Outside' is now partly open to women: they can go out, come and go, work outside, but not too far from home and never for too long. They are no longer shut up, but they are tied to the house with a lead which gives them an impression of freedom. Their geographical mobility has not increased to the same extent as man's. When a woman is mobile, she is following someone: *Ubi Gaius ibi Gaia.* Interestingly, the only women allowed by public opinion to travel widely are those who are professionally beautiful, whose job is to appeal to man's senses: dancers, actresses and film stars. They appear to have more spatial freedom, like the Greek or Chinese courtesans who were free to move while other women were closeted in their homes.

It is asserted that women are unsuited to executive posts, which require frequent travel and which would compel them to sacrifice their children and their family as a whole. This is in fact valid for women, but it does not apply to all. In any case, such arguments are not put forward against dancers or actresses, because women executives would be competing with men in the male sphere, whereas artists are attempting to please men. This is merely an instance of the old duality: inside for the woman, outside for the man, with the connotation of woman's inferiority and man's superiority. Nobody worries unduly about poor women leaving their countries and their families in order to work as maids in rich cities where there is a shortage of domestic staff. If every year thousands of Spanish, Portuguese and Greek young women went alone to take up well-paid and responsible jobs in London, Paris, Brussels or Berlin, there would be an outcry and it would not be thought 'right'. Similarly, during the Greco-Roman period, poor country women were not compelled to remain enclosed in their gynaeceum.

Almost everywhere women now have the right to vote and to stand for election. However, their share in public life remains much less than that of men, even in such countries as the Soviet Union, where today they have great educational and economic opportunities. Thus there is more difference between the civic activities of men and women in developed countries today than there was in the Germanic, Scandinavian or Gallic tribes and peoples before the Roman conquest.

2 Demography

A demographic revolution has been in progress for over a century. Revolutions need not be violent or man-made, they may be produced by the cumulative effects of social processes. Witness, for instance, the dramatic change which has occurred in the life expectation of women, particularly over the last fifteen years, as the result of a slow demographic transformation whose origins can be traced to the mid-nineteenth century and whose effects are truly revolutionary. This change is irreversible, and the course of women's lives, particularly in developed countries, has broken away from the mould in which it was cast thousands of years ago. This change is qualitative as well as quantitative – a fact public opinion has not yet grasped. Women themselves fail to realise that not only has their life-span been extended, but that this extension will necessarily affect the use they make of their whole lives. This lack of individual awareness is not surprising, since demographic facts have always been subject to misinterpretation. The history of demography itself is riddled with erroneous analyses made at the time of major changes in population structure.

Quite rightly, demography long ago adopted the convention of analysing male and female data separately. Since the eighteenth century, when the first efforts were made to establish this science, differences between the sexes in terms of birth rate, life expectation and death rate were noted and recorded. It was soon realised that there were more male than female births. The norm which is constant over time and place is a hundred and five male for each one hundred female births. It is a popular myth that this ratio increases after each war. In fact recorded deviations are slight, remaining within the range of 103·5 to 106·5 male per 100 female births. These variations are too small for wars to have significantly influenced them. The ratio of male to female births is higher among the stillborn: 120 to 100. Therefore it appears to follow logically that there should be more men than women in the world. In fact, the opposite is true today, and it is almost certain that in the total population of the world women exceed men. While this is true of our times, it is unlikely to have always been so.

Countries with a larger male population than female

The demographic data of some countries show a numerical predominance of the male over the female population. In this category one should single out such highly developed countries as Australia, Canada and New Zealand, where the excess male population is easily accounted for by immigration patterns. Their immigration policies attract a majority of men, predominantly young and unmarried, who venture out to settle in a new country. At the beginning of the century the United States experienced the same phenomenon. A corollary of this male predominance in countries attracting young immigrants is the low proportion of working women employed outside the home. The higher the ratio of young men to women in the population, the fewer women seek remunerative employment. Thus at the peak of immigration to the United States the percentage of working women was half that of European countries, for example, in Germany, when 300,000 single men emigrated towards the end of the nineteenth century, leaving behind an excess of single women seeking employment on the labour market.

Apart from countries with immigration policies and high living standards, there is a fairly large number of states which at the moment have a slightly greater male than female population. This is the case in many African nations – Gambia, Ghana, South Africa, United Arab Republic, Madagascar, Zanzibar, Upper Volta and Tunisia; in the Middle East – Iran, Iraq, Jordan and Syria; in the Far East – Cambodia, Ceylon, Burma, Malaysia, Korea, Thailand, the Philippines and, above all, India. At the last Indian census, held in 1964, 224 million men were registered against only 211 million women. Several Latin-American countries belong to this category – Cuba, Costa Rica, Panama, Venezuela (which alone attracts immigrants) and the Dominican Republic. This list calls for several comments:

First, the accuracy of the census may be doubted in predominantly rural countries whose people are in the main illiterate. In

45

any of these, registers of births and deaths are far from reliable.

Secondly, it will be noted that many of the countries listed are Moslem. In most, since women are segregated, it is the man of the house who has to register their existence. Possibly the disregard in which women are held influences the census by reducing the estimate of their numbers.

Thirdly, it is important to note that in many of these countries the average life span or life expectation is still very low. Life expectation at birth is calculated from actuaries' tables which show what percentage of a hundred thousand people born in one year survive each additional year in any given population. In many countries where there are more males than females, life expectation at birth is less than forty years. Thus a male child in Upper Volta has at birth a life expectancy of thirty-two years, whereas that of a female child is thirty-one years. In India the average life expectation is forty years and in many Latin American countries it does not exceed forty-five years.

Because of the greater number of male births, there are more men than women under the age of forty in all these countries. It is only when the life expectation of a country exceeds this age that women are more numerous than men. In other words, while male mortality rates are higher than female ones at all ages, this is particularly marked after forty. One can thus conclude that when a population has a low life expectation, the proportion of men and women is roughly equal.

Lastly, one must never forget that poor countries in which malnutrition and illiteracy are widespread have extremely high rates of infant mortality and also high rates of female mortality in childbirth.

Contemporary male and female life-expectations

Before moving on to the demographic situation in modern industrialised societies, we should remember that this terrible picture of the conditions prevailing in underdeveloped regions is little

In the past, the major cause of death among women aged twenty-five to thirty was childbirth. The risks are horrifyingly shown in this seventeenth-century picture of a Caesarian operation which was, of cours performed without anaesthetic.

different from the state of our own countries less than a centur ago.

During the eighteenth century and the beginning of the nine teenth, life expectation was no higher in western Europe than now is in Upper Volta or India. Among the older age group women barely outnumbered men. Parish registers provide informa tion from which age pyramids can be constructed for each Euro pean country in the seventeenth or eighteenth centuries. Suc pyramids show that the small group of people who lived into ol age included roughly the same proportion of men and womer Furthermore, this group was generally composed of members o the aristocracy or the wealthy middle class. Their small number and high social rank account for the respect with which they wer treated. While men were killed off at all ages in wars and by disease to which they are more prone than women, the danger of femal mortality was concentrated in the child-bearing period. Aroun thirty years of age, twelve per cent more women died than mer It is not from these dusty parish registers alone that one ca estimate the price women paid for motherhood, but also fror popular culture and folklore. All fairy tales are full of Cinderella and Snow-Whites who lost their own mothers and were persecute by step-mothers. History confirms these legends: diaries an chronicles are full of widowers who have remarried once or severa times on the death of their young brides in childbirth. In som cases this succession of remarriages amounted almost to polygam over time. The widower who used to be a stock character in histor has nearly disappeared today. The risk of death in childbirth ha been drastically reduced since Pasteur's time with the developmen of sterilisation and antiseptics, and the progress in gynaecolog and obstetrics. The puerperal fevers which alone were responsibl for the great majority of these deaths have been eliminated.

When saved from this killer, women have proved more resistan than men to diseases and stress. In the past, nature seems to hav balanced male and female mortality. This equilibrium has bee upset by medicine, which has found it easier to minimise th

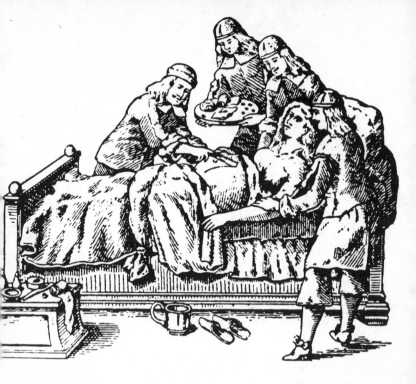

dangers of childbirth for women than to reduce men's tendency to go to war or to indulge in excesses! Thus alcoholism, road accidents, overwork or suicide are now the main causes of high mortality among men. The small margin of male superiority in the birth rate is not enough to outweigh these factors and guarantee parity in male and female death rates.

This difference between the sexes is increasing in developed countries. While in India women's life expectation is lower than that of men, in the developed world they are surviving longer and longer and outliving their men. It is therefore of the greatest importance to note that since the beginning of the century the life expectation of women has increased by a span of twenty to thirty-five years in the most industrialised countries.

Table 2:1 Male and female mortality at various ages in contemporary Italy

Age in years	Males	Females
	(per 10,000 in each age group)	
13	227	123
18	477	197
25	451	219
35	701	418
40	1009	637
45	1339	827
50	2150	1311
55	3316	1816
60	4658	2523
65	5677	3598

Table 2:2 Life expectation in years, of women in Great Britain

1844	42
1880	44
1890	47·2
1910	52·4
1920	59·6
1930	62·9
1950	71·5
1960	74·1
1966	74·7

Table 2:3 Life expectation at birth

Country	Women	Men
Netherlands	75·9	71·1
Sweden	75·7	71·6
Norway	75·5	71·3
France	75·1	68·0
Federal Germany	75·1	68·0
Switzerland	74·8	69·5
Denmark	74·6	70·3
Great Britain	74·2	68·1
Canada	74·1	68·8
Australia	74·1	67·9
USSR	74·0	67·0
New Zealand	73·7	68·4
United States	73·7	68·8
Belgium	73·5	67·7
Japan	72·9	67·7
Italy	72·2	67·2
Spain	71·9	67·3
Finland	71·5	64·9
Poland	70·5	64·8
Argentina	69·5	63·7
China	65·6	61·3
Yugoslavia	65·5	62·4
Mexico	57·9	55·1
Chile	53·8	49·8
Brazil	45·5	41·8
India	40·5	41·8
Africa (average)	41·0	39·9
Togo	38·5	31·6
Upper Volta	31·0	32·0

The effects of women's greater longevity

The figures in table 2:3 show the spectacular impact of development on average life expectation. However, it is in the post-war years that this increase in women's life-span has been most marked. Nor does it seem to have reached its limit in some countries where women already outlive men. Thus in France the latest estimates would place the life expectation of women above seventy-six years. But it does seem that certain highly industrialised countries, like the United States, have reached a ceiling due to a slight increase in mortality above the age of sixty and consequently to a lowering of the average life expectation among the very old.

It was thus in the shortest time interval that the greatest extension in women's life-span took place. Very soon the norm for women will have exceeded seventy-five years in many countries. A corollary of this prolongation is the increased number of widows in all societies In contemporary times women almost always end their lives alone, not only because they have a greater longevity, but also because most marry men older than themselves. This social convention further accentuates the disparity of life expectation between married partners.

In all societies with high living standards there is therefore an excess of women in the older age groups. This surplus is even greater and more widely distributed throughout the age cohorts in the countries which had heavy losses in the Second World War. There was a dramatic lack of men in a country such as the USSR, which in 1960 registered twenty million more women than men. This disequilibrium was slowly corrected by the boom in the post-war birth rate. At present the two sexes are equally represented in the age group under thirty-five. Nevertheless there was still a surplus of fifteen million women in the total population of 1967. These fifteen million 'spare' women of over forty years of age have had to pay a personal price for this shortage of men, a price which included widowhood, spinsterhood, loneliness, and sacrifices in bringing up fatherless children. This demographic disequilibrium

should not be forgotten in considering the strikingly high proportion of women in certain occupations, mainly in non-manual ones
where they represent fifty-four per cent of employed personnel.
Before drawing any conclusion about female superiority from this
percentage, it must be corrected to take account of their numerical
superiority in the population. Nor is Russia the only country where
war losses led to an excess of women. Poland, East Germany and
the Federal Republic were in the same position. In the latter there
were 4·5 million women in excess of the number of men by 1950;
ten years later this surplus had only been reduced to 3·5 million.
In Britain there are still 1·8 million more women than men and in
France 1·3 million.

The female life-cycle

It is necessary to bear in mind the different periodicities in the lives
of men and women. The existence of every woman is made up of
successive physiological stages which subdivide her life-span. Not
only is the difference between these phases experienced subjectively,
it is apparent in the body: puberty, defloration, maternity, menopause. The autopsy of an anonymous male body would merely
indicate his approximate age and whether he had reached puberty.
It would not reveal if he had ever had sexual intercourse or fathered
a child. From his puberty – a stage negotiated slowly, unlike the
girl's – to his death, man's physical life represents an unbroken
continuum. However, the autopsy of a similarly unknown female
body would provide a more detailed profile of her sexual development: degree of sexual maturity, virginity, childlessness or number
of births, menopause. Indeed each stage of hormone and genital
development brands itself suddenly and indelibly on her body.
One day, at a certain time, she becomes mature; one day, at a
certain time, she loses her virginity; one day, at a certain time, she
becomes a mother. And each time an ineradicable trace is left on
her body. Societies have always attached great importance to these
successive phases and devised ceremonies to mark some of them.

A counterpart of this awareness is the reluctance of public opinion to accord the title of woman to those females who have not experienced certain phases, for example, to the spinster or the childless. They may be of the female sex, but in the eyes of many they belong to it less than 'true women' do. In fact the nun is just as much a woman as the mother of ten children, in the same way that Don Juan was no more of a man than Saint Francis of Assisi. Yet it is her relationship with man rather than with the world at large which is always implicit in male definitions of woman. Even in our industrialised countries, which have moved so far from the primitive way of life, she is viewed in terms of her gynaecological rather than her intellectual development. Her life is thus subdivided to the detriment of its continuity: childhood, adolescence, youth, marriage, motherhood, middle age punctuated by the menopause and followed by old age. Until now the period of fecundity and reproduction has been the kernel of femininity, while the other phases of female life have often been presented or experienced as nothing more than the prologue or epilogue to this apotheosis which justifies her life. Thus Nietzsche summed up woman as 'a problem solved by pregnancy'.

Women have always lived through these consecutive stages and thus led several successive lives. However, recent fundamental changes have little by little altered this pattern of life, modified the allocation of roles and attached new values to the different phases and to the relations between them. This has been the case in industrialised countries, particularly in the 'fifties and 'sixties.

All these changes originate from improved hygiene, better living standards and the progress of medicine.

All of them have altered the focal point of woman's life: the time devoted to maternity has declined both absolutely and relatively in importance.

All of them have led to a dissociation of the former interconnexion between procreation and sexual intercourse.

All these changes are cumulative and compel us to reassess the life and the status of women.

Longer sexual life

The purely physiological aspects of this evolution seem to elude sociological or demographic explanation.

First, there has been a general lowering of the age of female puberty in developed countries. This is particularly striking in Scandinavia, where it used to be approximately fifteen at the beginning of the century and where the norm is now in the vicinity of twelve to thirteen years of age. A change of the same magnitude is taking place in the United States, and a lesser one in other countries in western Europe.

Secondly, the age at which menopause starts has progressively receded. According to documentary evidence, the average age for its onset in the eighteenth century was thirty-six in Europe and North America, whereas it is now about fifty. Gynaecologists who have practised for the last twenty years have unanimously noted this prolongation of female hormone activity. This anecdotal evidence has been corroborated statistically: women who were

Tristis Hiems senium nobis designat, et ætas.
Sera solet niuibus sæpe rigere suis.

Peace and security is reflected in this
happy family scene by Crispin de
Passe (1540–1629), but the harsh fact
was that only one child in two
reached the age of fourteen.

menstruating at fifty-two or fifty-three were the exception before
the Second World War, but are becoming more and more common.

This could perhaps be put down to better nutrition, improved
hygiene or a more active life. The exact cause is still unknown. In
this connexion the profound influence of socio-economic and
socio-cultural factors on human physiology should be borne in
mind. There is no such thing as eternal and unchanging womanhood. The increase in woman's life-span has not merely tacked on
years to her old age. It has delayed just that symptom which was
traditionally viewed as the end of youth. Not that the menopause
should in fact be considered as the prelude to old age. On the
contrary, many women are more active, less lethargic and in better
spirits in the years which follow it. Nevertheless the extension of
female fertility in developed countries during the last twenty years
is the more noteworthy for being a wholly unintended consequence
of the rise in living standards. The precise reasons for its occurrence
are still relatively unknown. It goes without saying that this picture
does not take into account the change induced by hormone treatment to prolong femininity, although this practice is fashionable in
some countries and in some circles.

Younger age at marriage
Another recent trend is the steady reduction of girls' age at marriage. The accuracy of official records during the last century made
it possible to ascertain the average age of men and women at
marriage. Such figures show marked national variations. Thus in
Europe it is Frenchwomen who marry earliest, and Irish women
latest. Since the end of the last war an overall decrease in the
age of brides has taken place, particularly if one excludes remarriages (of the divorced and widowed). At present the average
age on first marriage in the United States is 21·5 years. In other
countries this systematic decrease is also the rule. Far from being
predictable, this trend contradicts expectations that increases in
women's education and training would make them delay marriage.
Such has not been the case, for although young women everywhere

Women make younger mothers today than
formerly: indeed, most of them have had a
their children by thirty (see figure 3).

study over increasingly longer periods, they nevertheless marry at
earlier ages. The popular myth that it was our grandmothers who
really married young is disproved by facts. In France, where traditions favoured early marriage for girls, the average age of brides
(remarriages included) has been reduced by three years during the
last century, from twenty-six to twenty-three. However, in Sweden
where the age on marriage was relatively high, it has only taken
twenty years for the same decrease to occur.

In Latin countries such as Spain or Italy, marriage was traditionally postponed until the bride could contribute a dowry or at
least a trousseau, and until the bridegroom had a steady job. In
regions like Calabria or Sicily long engagements are still found
which do not result in marriage until the *corredo* has been put
together penny by penny and bit by bit over the years. Even so the
age of brides has been decreasing in Latin countries since 1960.
In Italy, for example, the records for 1960 show that 21·8 per cent
of brides were less than twenty-one years old and that 25·7 per
cent were aged between twenty-five and thirty. Only four years
later those marrying before twenty-one constituted 25·5 per cent
and those marrying between twenty-five and thirty were 23·2 per
cent of the total. The same trend is found in Great Britain, Holland,
Belgium, Germany, and even in Switzerland where late marriages
used to be customary.

The occurrence of marriage itself has slightly increased and the
percentage of spinsters diminished accordingly. Thus in England
if the number of married women between fifteen and forty-nine
out of one thousand women in 1911 is taken as the base 100, this
increases to 105 in 1931 and even more rapidly after the Second
World War to 133 in 1951 and 139 in 1966.

There are many reasons accounting for the greater frequency of
marriage and the decrease in the age at which it takes place. It
seems clear that the greater sexual precocity of the young plays an
important part, intensified or perhaps even provoked by the mass
media, with their insistence on the cult of youth, an idealised age
which appears to embody all the fashionable tenets of beauty,

Table 2 : 4 Average age of Swedish girls
on marriage

NOTE

Years	Average age on marriage
1941-5	26·1
1946-50	25·8
1951-5	25·3
1956-60	24·6
1961-5	23·7
1966	23·3

vitality and desirability. Moreover, the idea of marriage itself has been completely transformed. From being a financial bargain, an investment in social stability and a pact to perpetuate the line, it has largely become two people's attempt to perpetuate their love. Never has marriage been taken more seriously, never have young couples looked forward so much to their union. Marriage today is more complete and more durable than ever before, despite the outcry of those who see it as a fragile structure threatened by divorce and separation. A comparison with the real rather than the imagined past will show that the average married couple in the eighteenth century had to live only eighteen years together, whereas today they have forty years to share.

Any investigation of women's problems must emphasise that if today girls marry according to free choice of their hearts, this represents a very recent development and remains the prerogative of those living in developed countries. In other societies, while great efforts have been made to extend this freedom to women, governments like that of India admit their inability to eradicate traditional customs. Arranged marriages remain the norm.

It is interesting to note that women's attitudes to marriage in developed and underdeveloped countries are diametrically opposed. In industrialised societies the greater freedom enjoyed by young girls enables them to marry according to their inclination and earlier than was once usual in the more restrictive atmosphere of 1900. On the other hand, in many countries of the Third World, such as India, Burma and all the Moslem communities, the girl who dreams of emancipation longs to marry as late as possible. It is traditional for her to marry at the end of childhood or even during infancy. In several of these countries there is a growing awareness of the immorality of forced marriages at a tender age and a realisation that this custom prevents women from bettering themselves. It used to be common in Moslem countries to see the most brilliant pupils of secondary schools vanish at fifteen, quitting the studies in which they excelled for a marriage they did not want. This put an end to their education – they were never heard of again.

Hence the concern of several governments to establish a minimum marriageable age for women – and hence the laws passed on this subject in Algeria, Tunisia and the United Arab Republic. In the most advanced sections of the populations in those countries which are becoming increasingly progressive, girls wish to delay marriage at least until they are adult. They are beginning to protest more or less forcefully against this direct passage in adolescence from paternal control to the domination of an unknown or little-known husband.

As a result of contrary changes in the two different types of society, the average age at which women marry is tending towards a common norm. On the one hand, girls in Europe, North America, Australia, New Zealand and the more advanced sections of Latin-American populations tend to marry younger than before, generally between the ages of twenty and twenty-one. On the other hand, girls in Africa, in the Middle and Far East, as their countries develop, acquire the right to marry a little later and increasingly according to their own choice. Nevertheless, for them the average age on marriage remains extremely low. By the time they are twenty the great majority is married and has usually been so for several years. Statistics may be misleading since they only register legal marriage, and not traditional marriage. For instance, in Algeria a law making sixteen the minimum age of marriage for women was passed in 1963, but this has done nothing to prevent secret weddings under the *fatiha* (Moslem custom) involving girls of twelve or thirteen years of age. When they reach sixteen, their position is 'regularised' at a registry office. Thus in 1967 more than three-quarters of Algerian women were already married by the age of twenty. The situation is even more tragic in India where girls are wed before puberty and the engagement of children to marry is still common.

It is with reference to such countries where the young girl has no rights of her own, where the child is thrown into the arms of a husband who could be her father, that the United Nations Commission on the Status of Women submitted to the General

Assembly a 'declaration on the elimination of discrimination against women', which was adopted in November 1967. Article 6, paragraph 3 of this declaration states that:

Child marriages and engagements to marry made on behalf of girls before puberty shall be prohibited and effective measures, including legal provisions, shall be adopted to establish a minimum age for marriage and to make obligatory the official registration of marriage.

This resolution was not binding for the governments of member countries, but even so India wished to weaken it further by an amendment adding the words 'in so far as possible'. Clearly it will not be in the 1970's that any girl in the world will be free to marry at the age she wants to.

Two versions of the same ceremony.
Below The Palace of Weddings, Moscow.
Left An Indian wedding.

In the past women submitted to childbearing; they could not choose motherhood.
A typical seventeenth-century childbirth scene by Abraham Bosse.

Infant mortality

It is common knowledge that there has been a recent and steady decrease in infant mortality (defined as the death of children during their first year of life). However, the repercussions of this trend on women are less familiar. Generally this decrease is seen as a testimony to progress in hygiene and preventive medicine. On the other hand it has contributed to the population explosion in disrupting the former equilibrium between birth and death rates. The threat of overpopulation to the world as a whole has overshadowed its impact on individuals and particularly on the mother-child relationship.

This relationship has been transformed by the triumph of medical science over the low survival prospects of the newborn. For centuries even in our own part of the world, even in the most opulent homes, attended by physicians, filled with servants and counting a wet-nurse on the staff, children still died at an early age. Roughly one child in two did not reach his fourteenth birthday, the large majority of those who died living for less than twelve months. In such circumstances how could maternal feelings be what they are today? Each child appeared to have small odds in nature's stakes, which crowded the field so that a few might finish the race. By producing many children, the mother resigned herself to being the instrument of this natural design, which she was often tempted to call Providence. She did not analyse this design or rebel against it; children were given without her asking and taken away despite her pleading, so that anything other than resignation would have been useless.

Sometimes the mother was anguished, sometimes – according to many chronicles – she was almost indifferent, or displayed an animal resignation which passed for indifference. Tears and prayers at the death of an infant were cut short; it would have been unseemly to mourn such losses. Often the father did not grieve, or else was more upset at the loss of an heir than at the death of a human being. Among themselves women discussed this prob-

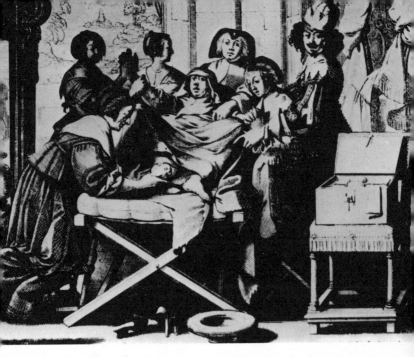

ability with a cold-bloodedness which today would shock by its cynicism. Thus in the seventeenth century a young mother of solid bourgeois background entertaining the respectable wives of judges who formed her circle of acquaintances was congratulated on her latest offspring. She answered that in future she meant to sleep apart, as she already had 'five little monsters who cried unceasingly'. 'My child, you are a fool' was the reply, 'before they are big enough to be a real nuisance, you will have lost half or perhaps all of them'. This quote from *Les Caquets de l'accouchée* was meant to illustrate rather than ridicule the attitudes of solid middle class women. It shows that women's familiarity with pregnancy was accompanied by a sense of alienation from the whole reproductive process that reduced them to mere instruments of destiny. Therefore one cannot even talk of mothers loving or not loving their infants; these words cannot have today's meaning. Writings of the past confirm that what we mean by maternal love is a modern invention inseparable from mastery over survival. Today each woman may consider pregnancy as a project which ninety-eight times out of a hundred will achieve completion and result in a child who will almost certainly survive her. She can look forward beyond the pregnancy itself; she is no longer the instrument of an attempt, but the mistress of a plan. She can look beyond delivery to the upbringing of a child. Consequently her role is becoming less restricted to child-bearing and more concerned with the upbringing of children. Until recently – indeed even now in some of the poorest countries – women submitted to reproduction rather than planning motherhood. They were always serving life and always frustrated by death. Their bodies, their time, and their future was not their own. They were the unwitting players of a game where the stakes had to be great because the losses were high.

Nowadays inflated birth rates lead to a fear of overcrowding. By contrast the recent past appears to have been a time of scanty populations thinly distributed over the surface of the earth. This is to forget the other side of the coin – the fecundity which was the counterpart of infant mortality. Women alone paid in body and in mind the price that nature imposed – to have fewer children than we do, our great-grandmothers put more of them into the world. This necessarily changed the meaning of motherhood. Let each reader count how many pregnancies her four great-grandmothers totalled between them. It is likely to be a difficult task, since only the children who outlived their parents are usually remembered. Research is needed to reconstruct the lives of these ancestors. It shows that, unless they were widowed early, succumbed to illness or became sterile, they passed their prime in reproduction. Only detailed family trees enable us to ascertain how many infants they lost. I have investigated the records of my own four great-grandmothers – two of whom were French, one from Alsace, the other from the south; one was German from Württemberg; the fourth lived in Guernsey. Their social status ranged from the working class to the opulent bourgeoisie. Between them they lost ten children in infancy. Interestingly it was the richest of them who lost most. Since one of them had been widowed early and never remarried, this presumably lowered the total.

The reduction of infant mortality has not had the same impact on men as on women. For the woman, procreation and sexual life no longer coincide. Sexual intercourse no longer necessarily entails motherhood and is no longer associated with fecundity – an association which was so close in the past that the sexual life of a couple was either cursed or blessed by offspring, depending on their interpretation of an event they could not control. The disengagement of the sexual act from procreation gives it an existence in its own right. Gradually it is seen as a source of pleasure whose enjoyment is not only normal, but even considered as a right. To previous generations this idea would have been deeply shocking and it is far from universally accepted even now. In many countries it is still referred to disparagingly as women's sexual 'forwardness'. In fact this modern trend is an inevitable consequence of the dissociation of sexual intercourse and fertility.

The moment medical techniques held death in check they were applied to the control of life. They disrupted the association between pleasure and procreation which had been indistinguishable in the sexual life of women. The purpose was not to increase pleasure, but to give humanity mastery over life after having achieved a victory over death. The growth of knowledge made enlightened decisions possible and forward planning feasible – family planning is rooted in the freedom to choose. No longer connected with reproduction, sensual pleasure became a new territory for women to explore and was no longer fraught with dangers or overlaid with the moral justification of continuing the human race. We have hardly begun to see the consequences of this revolution. Perhaps more than any other scientific advance, this has incited a stream of polemics precisely because the subject has been so encumbered with myths and moralising. It has been argued that violating Nature's secret would strip life of all that was sacred. However, it is we who attribute the notion of sanctity to Nature, not Nature to us. Undoubtedly the future will see an intensification of this debate, not only in Catholic circles, but among thinkers of all persuasions, since we shall not cease to study the phenomenon of life and since we shall continue to disrupt tradi-tional associations, we shall only add fuel to controversy. Indeed we shall be increasingly pressed by the population explosion to push back further the frontiers of our knowledge. We shall be forced to reconsider the traditional areas of human conduct to which conventional morality was applied. Nevertheless we shall retain a sense of awe in the face of two mysteries: that of birth and that of love. The way in which women envisage their sexual life (which I would prefer to call their love life) has changed and will go on changing.

Above all it is the feminine view of motherhood which has altered. Fatalism, resignation, passivity or a brave acceptance of fate – call it what you will – this attitude of woman who had blindly to submit to fecundity and fulfil the obscure designs of nature has disappeared, or rather is disappearing with the abrupt decline in infant mortality and with its logical corollary, family planning.

The decrease in infant mortality
This decrease has been very rapid indeed, as inspection of recent mortality rates from many countries shows. There is not even any need to make comparisons with the last century. Data from countries with available statistics have been compiled for the years 1900, 1935 and either 1963 or 1964. It is striking that in 1935 the infant mortality rates were as high in parts of Europe as they are now in the poorest underdeveloped countries or even higher. Yet that was only a generation ago.

Earlier motherhood

In developed countries there have only been small variations in the birth rate in the recent past. All such societies experienced the baby boom of 1945-55, followed by a slight reduction in number of births since 1965, occurring whether or not family planning was a long established practice.

However, a study of the statistics for the last twelve years shows a tendency which has not been sufficiently stressed until now. Increasingly women have more children at the beginning of their marriage and fewer after ten years of wedlock. In other words, more children are being born to very young mothers and fewer of them to mothers over thirty years of age. As the standard of living improves, so does the tendency for countries to provide family planning centres, and yet the younger the mothers become. Some of those who feared the effects of the pill have been saying for years that one great danger would be the postponement of maternity by women. They expected an increase in the number of children born to older mothers, with all the well-known accompanying draw-backs, for instance, a greater frequency of chromosomic defects in children born to the over-forties. These allegations are contra-dicted by a breakdown of births according to the age of mothers in the countries where contraception is available. Indeed, in countries where the pill can be prescribed, it would seem as if young women, marrying earlier than their mothers did, hurry to have a family. It is only when they have two or three children that they seem to use methods of family planning in order to limit their fertility from then on. The fertility rate of women over thirty years of age continues to decrease in comparison with that of thirty or even ten years ago. On the other hand this rate has steadily increased for women less than twenty-five years old.

Very few countries provide birth statistics allowing for com-parison over time according to age of mother, but those which do are among the most developed. The change is worth recording and is particularly striking in Scandinavia and the United States, though not limited to these countries. Thus in England the fertility rate (or number of births per thousand women in each age group) has increased more markedly among young women. Between 1954 and 1964 it passed from 22·6 to 42·3 for mothers between fifteen and nineteen years. For those between twenty and twenty-four, it has changed from 136·1 to 179·5, an increase of 43·4 per thousand. For the age group between twenty-five and twenty-nine, the

Table 2:5 Number of deaths of infants under one year of age per thousand births

Country	1900	1935	1963/4
Austria	209	86	29·2
Belgium	145	83	27·2
Bulgaria	-	146	32·9
Czechoslovakia	-	111	22·1
Denmark	-	64	19·1
Eire	-	70	26·7
Finland	142	68	17·0
France	164	71	22·1
Federal Germany	187	66	23·8
Great Britain	153	59	23·4
Greece	-	113	35·8
Hungary	235	136	40·0
Italy	176	103	35·5
Yugoslavia	-	139	76·0
Netherlands	158	37	14·8
Norway	-	40	16·9
Poland	-	136	47·7
Portugal	--	139	69·0
Romania	216	181	48·6
Spain	164	125	37·9
Sweden	102	75	14·2
Switzerland	149	49	19·0
USSR	258	75	28·0
Argentina	-	-	60·0
Brazil	-	-	-
Canada	-	67	24·7
Chile	-	241	114·2

Country	1900	1935	1963/4
Columbia	-	-	83·3
Cuba	-	-	37·7
Ecuador	-	-	89·9
Guatemala	-	-	91·6
Jamaica	-	-	39·5
Martinique	-	-	38·1
Mexico	-	-	64·5
Peru	-	-	83·3
United States	118	53	24·8
Venezuela	-	-	49·4
Australia	-	-	18·2
Gambia	-	-	79·4
Ghana	-	-	82·3
Guinea	-	-	32·5
India	-	162	81 *
Indonesia	-	-	74·7
Japan	-	110	23·3
Madagascar	-	-	76·3
Mozambique	-	-	83·8
New Zealand	-	-	19·0
Senegal	-	-	82·4
South Africa	-	-	Whites 33·6
			Asians 50·5
			Negroes 115·7
Thailand	-	-	37·9
Vietnam	-	-	29·3

* Incomplete data.

corresponding increase has been from 139 to 185, i.e. forty-six per thousand. On the other hand the group of mothers aged between thirty and thirty-five produced approximately the same number of children in 1964 as it did in 1954 – fifty in 1964 and 45·4 in 1954. For older age groups, that is mothers above thirty-five years of age, there has been a decrease in the average number of children born over the last ten years. The size of each cohort has no influence on these figures, since they are calculated on the basis of the number of births per thousand women within the cohorts. The fact that the young are more numerous than those of thirty years and more, because of the post-war baby boom, only increases the significance of the phenomenon.

Similarly, in the Netherlands the number of children (legitimate live births) per thousand women aged between thirty-five and thirty-nine was 121 in 1939, had shrunk to 101 in 1960 and only six years later had further diminished to 72·7, a decrease which may be attributed to the pill. A greater reduction has thus taken place in the six year period between 1960 and 1966 than in the twenty years between 1940 and 1960. For mothers aged forty years and over a decrease has been registered, from 28·5 per thousand in 1939 to 21·2 in 1960 and 13·8 in 1966. As this trend has not applied to younger mothers, the breakdown of births according to age of mother has completely changed since the war and in particular since 1960. Mothers aged under thirty account for an increasingly important proportion of the total number of births in the country. In the year 1939 women aged more than thirty had 87,471 children as against the 85,165 born to mothers under that age. In 1966 these positions were reversed, the over-thirties having 81,138 children compared with the 153,777 born to the under-thirties (i.e. nearly double).

A similar trend has also prevailed in France. Again, in each thousand it is mothers in the younger age groups who on average have had more children and the over-thirties fewer. The fertility rate has increased particularly among women aged between eighteen and twenty-two; it has decreased particularly for those aged

Table 2:6 Number of legitimate live births according to age of mother in the Netherlands

Year	under 25	25-29	30-34	35-39	over 40
1939	32,418	52,747	46,925	28,801	11,945
1960	52,982	78,826	57,677	34,306	12,108
1966	74,836	78,941	47,832	24,586	8,720

Table 2:7 Number (and percentages in brackets) of births according to age of mother in Sweden

Age	1954	1957	1960	1965	1966
Under 25	28,092 (29·6)	29,807 (30·9)	30,140 (32·2)	41,567 (39·3)	42,643 (40·4)
25-29	28,666 (30·2)	29,916 (31·1)	28,396 (31·0)	33,920 (32)	33,911 (32·2)
Over 30	38,051 (40·2)	36,595 (38·0)	32,147 (35·5)	30,369 (28·7)	28,838 (27·4)
Total births	94,809 (100)	96,318 (100)	90,683 (100)	105,856 (100)	105,392 (100)

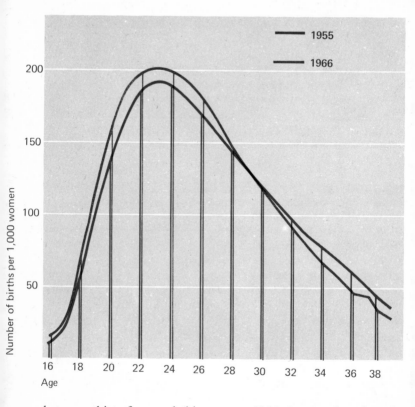

Figure 1 Number of live births per 1,000 women according to age in France in 1955 and 1966

1955
1966

200

150

100

50

Number of births per 1,000 women

16   18   20   22   24   26   28   30   32   34   36   38
Age

between thirty-four and thirty-seven. If births are plotted against mother's age (ranging from sixteen to forty years) curves can be drawn for 1955 and 1966 respectively. By superimposing these curves the shift towards younger motherhood is made clear. The two lines intersect at the point corresponding to thirty years of age. This illustrates the recent trend towards concentrating maternities in the early years of married life rather than spacing them out. Moreover, the numerical predominance of the younger age group over the older (over-thirties) means – as in Holland – that the number of children born to young women under twenty-five increases absolutely as well as relatively.

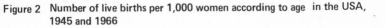

Figure 2   Number of live births per 1,000 women according to age in the USA, 1945 and 1966

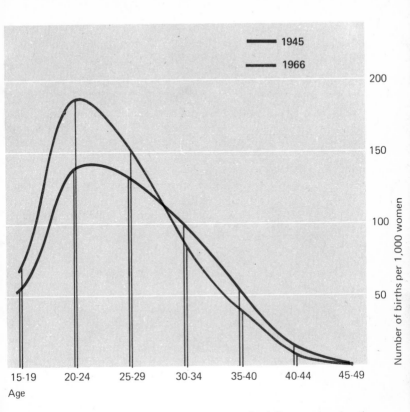

This trend seems even stronger in the United States, despite the stabilisation of the birth rate in 1966 and 1967. This has slightly offset the spectacular increase in number of births to young mothers, which reached its peak between 1955 and 1960. A table of births per age of mothers in 1945 and 1966 has been constructed. It shows that for the age group twenty to twenty-four, there have been fifty-three more births per thousand in 1966 than in 1945, whereas for the age group thirty to thirty-four there have been fifteen less. The drop in the fertility of the over-thirties has been uninterrupted during the last two decades. The increase in fertility among the very young together with their numerical importance accounts for the youth of American mothers. More than half of them have had their *last* child before their thirtieth birthday.

The change has been equally striking in Sweden, as table 2:7 shows. Numbers of births have deliberately been categorised under three age groups of mothers: under twenty-five, twenty-five to twenty-nine, and over thirty. The fertility rates for each group have changed completely over the last eleven years. While the middle category of women aged between twenty-five and twenty-nine continues to provide about thirty per cent of the total number of births in the country, those under twenty-five only accounted for 29·6 per cent of Swedish children born in 1954 but produced 40·4 per cent twelve years later. On the other hand the over-thirties register a fall from 40·2 to 27·4 per cent over the same period. The youth of Swedish mothers is even more spectacular than that of their Dutch counterparts, since it is women under twenty-five who account for this trend.

The Danish picture is very much the same. Very young women have more children. Thus from 1954 to 1966 the fertility rate increased by ten per cent for women between fifteen and nineteen, by eighteen per cent for those between twenty and twenty-four and by ten per cent for those between twenty-five and twenty-nine, while there has been a steady decrease for the age group over thirty.

Summary of change

It might be useful to sum up all the demographic material presented before analysing its consequences:

1 The life-span of women has been considerably extended: since the beginning of the century in developed countries they have added on average between twenty-five and thirty years to their expectation of life.

2 They outlive men and are consequently more numerous among the over-forties. Therefore the percentage of widows is constantly increasing.

3 They marry younger.

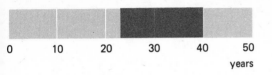

Figure 3   Period devoted to maternity in the average life of a woman in 1900

0   10   20   30   40   50

years

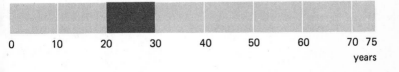

Period devoted to maternity in the average life of a woman in 1970

0   10   20   30   40   50   60   70 75

years

4 They no longer die in childbirth and hardly ever lose children in infancy.

5 They have slightly more children who survive them than did their mothers and grandmothers, but far fewer pregnancies.

6 Their fertility lasts longer than ever before: they menstruate at an earlier age and begin the menopause later in life, and yet their fertility rate is lower. Their reproductive and sexual activities are increasingly dissociated.

7 They have, particularly since 1960, tended to bear their children increasingly in their early youth and decreasingly after thirty years of age.

8 Approximately half of them, and more than half in some countries, have completed their family by the time they reach the age of twenty-six or seven. Thus when the youngest child starts school, the mother has forty years of life before her, whereas her grandmothers only had a life expectation of forty-five years in all.

9 The period of their life devoted to maternity in relation to total life expectation is shrinking (see figure 3).

This is a truly revolutionary change; in the past woman has always been defined by reference to her maternal role, yet at present the years devoted to maternity hardly add up to a seventh of her total life-span. From now on the longest phase in her life will be that which follows the completion of her family. In view of this, girls of every age should be brought up in the clear expectation of

having a long future ahead of them. Unfortunately this does not seem to be the case. I have tried the experiment of asking a group of young boys and girls between eighteen and nineteen years of age to write a description of a day in their future life at the age of fifty. While the boys were willing to co-operate, I never discovered what their projection into the future would have been, because the embarrassed and outraged reaction of the girls stopped the experiment. Amid tittering, the girls rapidly made it clear that the whole idea was absurd to them. They were all quite certain that they would be dead at that great age. While allowing that according to modern statistics one of them would die before fifty, I assured

Nowadays women live longer then men, so
that many of them end their lives alone.
Here, an old people's home in France.

77

them that the rest would not only reach this age, but exceed it by many years. At fifty they would be in their prime – could they not imagine how they would pass their time? The boys, ready to describe their imaginary future, were highly entertained by this female flutter. Thereupon one girl declared that she would much rather commit suicide than live so long and marched out of the room. This example was promptly followed by all the others, who broke up the meeting with giggles and excuses. Obviously they preferred to imagine dying twenty or thirty years earlier rather than lose a single hour thinking about a future in which they would no longer be seductive. They were able to see as far ahead as marriage and a baby or two or even three. They could imagine a professional life as a doctor, or an interior decorator, a journalist or a teacher, a psychologist or beautician, but only when young.

I have told this story to many people in several countries. Young girls have often confirmed that they would have been equally disturbed by the same question. Yet they begin adult life keen, bright, demanding, and competitive. But this leads to a dead end. When youth is over, they get along as best they can, in resignation or bitterness. They still identify with one image of woman and, unlike boys, cannot imagine that their personality may be expressed in other ways once the curtain has come down on the first act of the play.

3 Home and work

It is not demographic change alone which has transformed the life of women during the last twenty years. One of the main aspects of social evolution has been the increased employment of women in many countries and their redistribution in the occupational structure.

For centuries women were economically productive in the home. Nowadays their domestic productivity keeps shrinking. As we have seen, women used to supply the home with water; now it is available at the turn of a tap, and it is male plumbers, engineers and waterboard employees who assure its flow. Similarly when we switch on the electric light, we give employment to a whole series of male workers, whereas in the past women made candles and tended lamps. The Gospel refers to the wise virgin's care to supply her lamp with oil. The preserves formerly made by housewives are now mass produced by an industry which gives employment to many men. It is also male labour which produces the washing machines, vacuum cleaners and other domestic appliances which simplify housework. Increasingly the textile industry employs men rather than women. In the past, every stage of cloth making, spinning, wool carding, setting up the warp, weaving, cutting out and making up was carried out by women either in cottage industries or for their families. Gradually most of these female tasks have become mechanised and entrusted to male workers. Mechanisation had a similar impact on milling – when flour was ground by hand, it was women who did it; as soon as wind and water mills were invented, men took over. Many more instances of this process could be quoted. After mechanisation has taken place, there is always a shift from handicrafts and cottage industries based on the family to industry sited away from the home and largely employing wage-earners.

Thus if one tries to evaluate the contribution of women to the output of a country, it would be much smaller today than in the Middle Ages, when women produced as much as or even more than men. It would even be smaller than in the nineteenth or early twentieth century, since to the work performed by women in

80

agriculture, industry, commerce and domestic service, one could also have added their numerous productive and manufacturing activities in the home, before the coming of chemical, clothing and canning industries.

The economic role of the housewife diminished even more sharply after the Second World War. Increasingly everything is labour-saving, prepared 'ready for use' or ready-mixed in order to save her trouble. While in the recent past to have a woman in the home was an indispensable economic asset, in our time she has become a consumer, a shopper and a devotee of pre-packed products and of gadgets. Hence public opinion now stresses the psychological or moral significance of her *presence* in the home – her economic contribution no longer justifies it.

The only capacity in which the housewife retains a strictly economic value (quite apart from psychological considerations) is in looking after children, particularly in infancy. Indeed it is often more expensive for a young mother to work and pay for a nursery to mind her children than to do it herself. Even socialist countries have begun unobtrusively to revise the basic tenets laid down by Lenin whereby women were to be relieved of domestic and family duties to give them an equal chance of training and employment. The tacit reason behind this revision is that the cost to the state of providing crèches and day nurseries exceeds that of allowing young mothers to withdraw their labour from the economy during several years.

In all other respects the housewife has become marginal to the economy. Far from being an earner through her production in the home, she has become a spender in her demand for costly domestic appliances. Instead of reducing the household budget by her activity, she now increases it. Until recently men relied on a woman to keep house for them. Nowadays they can if need be buy pre-packed meals, have their washing done in a launderette and have their flat centrally heated. They can certainly do without women better than ever before, even if this might not be very pleasant.

Thus women have become slowly aware that if they wish to contribute to the well-being of their families, the best way to do so is by becoming wage-earners. Certainly in the home they can still be good cooks and dressmakers; this will gratify their families, but will not pay. To make one's own clothes, jams or preserves has almost become a leisure time pursuit, a hobby. It may give pleasure to those attached to the traditions of their childhood, but it does not increase the standard of living of the family. 'Do-it-yourself' has become psychologically valuable, but economically expensive. On the other hand the second wage that the wife can earn represents the means of securing a better house, better medical care in countries without a free health service, more luxurious holidays and above all the possibility for extending the children's education. All these assets could not be secured if women remained housewives. By working they can increase not only the family's welfare, but its social standing or at least that of the children. A growing number of women implicitly think along these lines, without having worked out the economics in detail, and decide to continue in employment after marriage. This attitude is largely

due to technological and economic change. It has not transformed
the traditional feminine outlook and has not sprung from dis-
content or rebellion.

However, other women go out to work for totally different
reasons which indicate a new state of mind. They are prompted
by the tediousnesss of housework, the isolation of the housewife,
their need for personal fulfilment, sometimes their sense of voca-
tion or the need to use their talents, gifts or training. One should
not underestimate this new development of female psychology,
which in some countries is leading to a reappraisal of the masculine
and the feminine roles in the home. Nevertheless, even without
changes in outlook, even if women retain traditional expectations,
a great many of them would be led to undertake paid work solely
because of the economic and demographic factors already outlined.
A growing number of mothers, having devoted several years to
their infants, are then anxious to go out to work. When one asks
working wives for the main reason which led them to take a job,
95 per cent cite the money earned. In itself this is unrevealing,
since men are also motivated by remuneration. In any case mone-
tary requirements are essentially relative – while one woman may
stay at home claiming that her husband earns quite enough money,
another whose husband brings home exactly the same wage will
say that she has to work because it is insufficient. The financial
motive is a blanket term which covers many other personal considerations as a pretext that outside work is for the sake of the
family's welfare. The woman who admits that she works for her
own sake, for the satisfaction she derives from it, is exceedingly
rare – although much quoted by magazines. Public opinion condemns her, because she stands for a new outlook. However, the
majority of women do not affront traditional attitudes, since they
only work for the sake of others – and yet they accept the requirements of a modern economy. They are therefore willing to see
their wage treated as a subsidiary income, although this notion
entails discrimination and is ultimately detrimental to women as
a group.

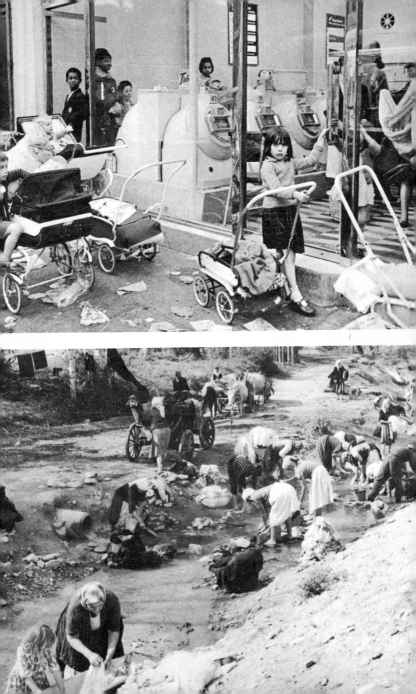

Increased demand for womanpower

While the housewife's role was losing its economic value, the need for womanpower in the economy was increasing. Since 1950 several countries have experienced an unprecedented economic growth rate. A well-known corollary of prosperity is the multiplication of jobs. In several countries, such as the United States, Germany and Sweden, the need for workers has resulted in an attempt to tap the unused resources of womanpower. This trend has been emphasised by the development of the tertiary sector (office work and service jobs) in all industrialised countries. Such work requires no physical strength and can be undertaken by women as well as by men. Recent statistics on the employment of women show that it is in the tertiary sector that a spectacular increase has taken place. The demand for womanpower has equalled and in some countries exceeded the supply of female workers, a fact which has contributed to the increase in part-time employment.

It is demographic factors which account to a great extent for the increased employment opportunities of women. The new lease of life women enjoy after the time devoted to maternity gives them a good twenty years in which to pursue a career. It would be

Menial office jobs are now mainly done
by women, as here in a Paris office.

85

a burden for society if mature women who represent a growing
proportion of the population remained inactive. As it is, the active
population is increasingly burdened, since the old live longer and
the young are compelled by the development of knowledge to
undertake extensive studies before entering the employment market.
According to some economists, our societies will be capable of
supporting a larger inactive population without retrenchment.
While this may be so in theory, in practice the leisure society is
still far away, except as a subject of conversation. We have not yet
experienced a drastic decrease in the ratio of the active to the total
population. Our societies are still involved in the production/con-
sumption race and our policies are to keep unemployment due to
automation in check. Full employment is still an ideal. It is even
more utopian to hope for a reduction in the ratio of active to
passive population coupled with a continuous rise in living standards. On the contrary, in most countries economic expansion has
increased the number of women workers.

Moreover, girls increasingly receive an extensive education, often
state-financed. If afterwards they do not work, society's investment
in their instruction brings no return – and the wisdom of having
educated them in the first place may be doubted. However, progress
is irreversible in our societies. Far from questioning the increased
education of women and considering a return to the days of
educational discrimination between the sexes, we are moving in
the opposite direction: the more educated young women are, the
more anxious they become to work and to devote themselves to a
career. Statistics from all over the world confirm this.

In these changed and changing circumstances a new climate of
opinion surrounds the problem of working women. There is not a
single country where this does not represent a controversial issue.
It is indeed a difficult one which cannot be simplified without risk
of distortion, and yet as a rule it is over-simplified.

The public is insufficiently informed about the position of
women on the labour market in the recent past and the present. It
is unaware of the numbers of working women, of the sharp

increase and distribution throughout the different sectors of the economy of these numbers, the impact of marital status, of age and level of instruction on employment, the discontinuity of some feminine careers, the low level of qualifications resulting from educational discrimination, and the inequality of pay and promotion. Public opinion knows very little, if anything, of all this.

It is the ignorance of basic facts in the context of recent economic and technological developments which enables public opinion to contend vainly that work for women is a purely moral problem. The question is always formulated in the absolute: '*Ought* a woman to work?', overlooking the fact that 'woman' has never existed and never will. There are only girls, spinsters, married women, educated ones, and untrained ones, mothers of large families and those of only children, peasants and town dwellers, widows, divorced and separated women, those who are capable of work and those who are not. To ask whether 'woman ought to work' is to posit a purely ethical problem, which can be solved without reference to the economic pressures of her environment. It is to assume that such pressures influence men, but have no impact on women. This moralistic approach which one meets in all countries, in the popular press and in public debate gives the erroneous impression that each woman is free to choose between paid employment and life at home. Man is never seen as being free, but is forced both morally and financially to work, whereas woman is alleged to have a total and untrammelled freedom to choose. She has therefore more liberty than man since her choice rests on purely ethical or religious principles. This convenient way of viewing reality is based on mere illusion. The activity of woman is determined by factors which outweigh her free will. It is useless to approach the subject of women working as a general ethical issue, settling it by taking sides – either condemning those who seek employment or despising those who do not. In democratic countries where work is not compulsory, there is only one answer: it is equally impossible for all women to be unemployed as for all of them to be employed.

Thus it is futile to categorise those who investigate the problem of working women into 'supporters' and 'critics'. Yet this is the way in which their statements are assessed, since the debate is loaded with emotion. The public's emotional attitude is in itself a social factor. Because of it, audiences and readers, male and female alike, will note none of the objective facts about women's work which have been presented. They will merely struggle to discover the bias of the speakers or authors, in order either to accuse them of denying female emancipation or of wishing to destroy femininity by imposing on it an inimical activity. In any case the moral debate summed up by the question 'Ought woman to work?' is highly artificial since it refers to a limited number of individual women. The so-called freedom to choose does not exist for spinsters – distinguished from 'real women', they are often relegated to the ranks of the pseudo-female because their existence interferes with popular over-simplification. Neither does this freedom exist for widows, nor for divorcees, nor for the numerous married women whose husbands earn too little to keep the home together. Freedom (or lack of it) hardly affects the married woman with no children, for she enjoys a kind of exemption which concedes her the right to work. Similarly when children are grown up, the moral objection vanishes and it is understood that their mother can go back to work. In fact there is only one group to which the debate applies in all its virulence, namely young mothers with small children. However, they are a very small minority of the female workforce: those who work while their children are under twelve years of age constitute only eight to fifteen per cent of working women, depending on the country (apart from eastern European countries).

Women are always presumed guilty
The clearest result of this controversy is the deep guilt feeling which haunts so many women today. Those who do not work blame themselves for vegetating. They feel that they are suspected of being incompetent, parasitic, out of date. They may react by feeling an overwhelming discouragement due to a sense of inferiority and culpability. Alternatively they may over-react by displays

of aggressive jealousy towards working women, accusing them of being bad mothers, bad wives or traitors to their sex. On the other hand those who work are haunted by this treason with which they are branded. If they leave a trace of dust on their furniture, if their husband grumbles, if their child has a bad school report or a sore throat, they tend to blame it on their job and to feel guilty.

This tension is widespread on both sides of the demarcation line between working and non-working women. It is not only useless, but downright harmful; it helps no one and prevents many women from feeling fulfilled. Yet it is an attitude encouraged in Catholic and Protestant countries alike, whether they possess a long tradition of working women or not. Indeed, concepts of the female role are set in rigid patterns which cannot change rapidly, because people insist on describing woman as the cornerstone of the family, the guardian of tradition and the defender of social stability. She is always represented as the mediator between past and present, while man sees himself as the mediator between the present and the future. While she is meant to conserve what is best in the past, he must build for the future. The faster society evolves, the more woman is required to assure its stability amid change. This is a difficult task which proves traumatic for many. Women are asked to be conservative and non-innovatory. At the same time, if they do not keep up with social change, they render themselves vulnerable, at least in economic terms. This accounts for the flagrant inadequacy of the training given to so many girls in all countries; they are given the palliative of diplomas in home economics and dressmaking certificates, which will do nothing for them when they need to work.

The subject of women working is currently overdramatised. The evils attributed to it are easy to find in the popular press. Thus in the same month the French press informed us that:

The increase in the divorce rate is due to wives working,
and that
The increase in children held back a year in school is due to mothers working.

In fact divorce rates are not increasing in France and indeed are much lower than in certain countries where the proportion of women at work is much less important. Although the French divorce rate was lower before the war, the percentage of women working at that time was higher than it is today. France, like Austria, Belgium or Italy, has significantly fewer female workers at present than in the first quarter of the century, for reasons which will be discussed later.

On the other hand, research conducted in Great Britain, the United States and France (in the latter in a study of 9,000 children in state schools) has repeatedly established that children whose mothers work generally perform better at school than those whose mothers stay at home. (One of the explanations of this finding is that in all countries the average level of education of working women is higher than that of housewives and in consequence it may be assumed that children benefit from a climate conducive to educational achievement.) Although these results have been published, they have had no influence; it is easier to accuse working mothers than to search for the real causes of failure in school.

Considered alone, the two examples quoted on the previous page may look like caricatures of public opinion but one could back them up with many more instances of the same attitude. This is the social background against which guilt feelings arise among working women. Indeed woman has never been truly viewed as an individual, a citizen endowed by the constitution with inalienable rights, but as part of the family unit. The family is no longer thought of as a dictatorship, but as a basic unit controlled by the husband, responsible for its relations with the outer world, and the wife, responsible for its internal affairs. Thus the idea of women working outside the home is still condemned by a majority of men (from fifty-six per cent in France to eighty-two per cent in the Netherlands). On the other hand a decreasing number of women object to female employment and a majority in its favour is appearing in a large number of countries. The difference between the attitudes of the sexes to this problem is very great, certain investigations show-

ing divergences of twenty-five to forty per cent between their respective opinions on this subject. Consequently the number of married couples who hold conflicting views in this respect must be considerable. This conflict appears greatest within the working class and least pronounced among the younger generation. Nevertheless a majority of male students still claim that after marriage their wife should remain at home, whereas an equally large majority of female students hope to work after marriage (sixty-eight per cent in the United States and eighty per cent in France hold this view).

An important component of male resistance to women working is that, in general, employment must be found outside the home. Thus the old patriarchal dichotomy remains, outside activities being still reserved for men and the home for women. This is confirmed by research showing that men look more favourably on women working if they can do so at home.

Husbands may see this as an acceptable compromise, but to women this 'solution' appears to have only disadvantages. To them it combines the worst of both worlds: tiredness and isolation, constant work in an enclosed place, no outside contacts, no work-mates, great difficulty in asserting one's rights, children under one's

Urbanisation has made life easier for
many women, but it brings with it its
own problems of loneliness and alienation.

feet, no break, no breathing space. Only women saddled with extreme guilt feelings at the thought of absenting themselves from home will agree to work at home. However, they are a negligible minority.

Before proceeding to a discussion of the numbers of women at work in various countries, one should note the persistence of an old myth, which still colours modern attitudes. This myth, that the need for women to work was only temporary and would vanish as soon as the economic situation improved, has been periodically upheld in Italy and Germany. This view used to be widespread in the nineteenth century when the Industrial Revolution replaced cottage industries by large factories employing thousands of women. Thus in Great Britain the employment of female operatives was denounced as a modern aberration which should be eradicated. In France the same sentiment was echoed by Michelet's attack on the 'unnaturalness' of female employment in factories. It seemed then that when order and prosperity prevailed, the pathological phenomenon of women at work would diminish and ultimately disappear. Even now many men retain this view, particularly among the working class. They frequently state that 'when things get better' or 'if things were properly organised' men will or would be paid enough for their wives not to need outside employment. This view itself is unrealistic since no woman can count on being protected by a man throughout her life. Not only is it utopian, it is economically unsound. The underlying assumption that if women did not compete for work, there would be no unemployment, is completely unfounded, as a study of female employment in various countries will show.

Married women at work

One of the most striking aspects of female employment is the recent change in the marital status and age composition of womanpower. This is a logical outcome of the demographic change referred to earlier and consists of:

An English cotton mill in the 1840s.
It was cheaper to employ women and
children than men.

1 A considerable increase in the number of married women at work, seen in the changed composition of the labour force.

2 A greater discontinuity in the careers of women: work before marriage, its interruption during the years devoted to motherhood, and its subsequent resumption.

3 The steady increase in the average age of women workers.

Marriage lasts longer than ever before. Once the children have grown up, their mother has many years of life before her. For these and other reasons already mentioned, an increasing number of married women work. Since the marriage rate has increased in most countries, it is therefore not surprising that the proportion of married women who work has grown accordingly. In the United States, France, Sweden and in Great Britain, married women con-

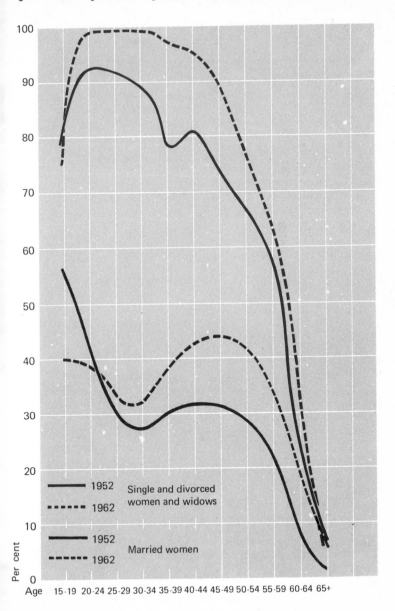

Figure 4 Percentages of working women according to age in the United Kingdom

1952 ——— Single and divorced
1962 - - - women and widows

1952 ——— Married women
1962 - - -

Per cent

Age 15-19 20-24 25-29 30-34 35-39 40-44 45-49 50-54 55-59 60-64 65+

Table 3:1 Percentage of married women (living with their husbands) of total womanpower

USA	52 in 1950	60 in 1960
Sweden	30 in 1950	55 in 1962
France	49 in 1954	53·2 in 1962
Great Britain	43 in 1955	50 in 1967

stitute the majority of the female labour force in recent times (see table 3:1).

A similar trend is noticeable in other countries. Thus the proportion in Norway has increased from twelve per cent in 1950 to twenty-five per cent in 1960 and in Sweden from sixteen per cent to twenty-five per cent in the same years. If one takes the percentage of married women to German womanpower in 1950 as base 100, this index has risen to 111 in 1957 and 120 in 1962. Even in Holland where so few married women work the rate has risen from 7·1 per cent in 1955 to 18·4 per cent in 1964.

This evolution is illustrated in figure 5, which unfortunately does not go beyond 1960 or 1962. The infrequency of national census and the delays involved in the analysis and publication of results account for this. However, the figure indicates a clear trend which has become even more accentuated in the 'sixties.

Discontinuity in working life
This is a recent problem which can only be aggravated in the future. Not so long ago the only women who worked were those who had to, i.e.:
1 Those who were not supported by men: spinsters, widows, divorced women and abandoned wives.
2 Those married women whose husband's wages were insufficient or irregular.
3 Finally, married women who worked alongside their husbands

Figure 5 The proportion of married women among working women

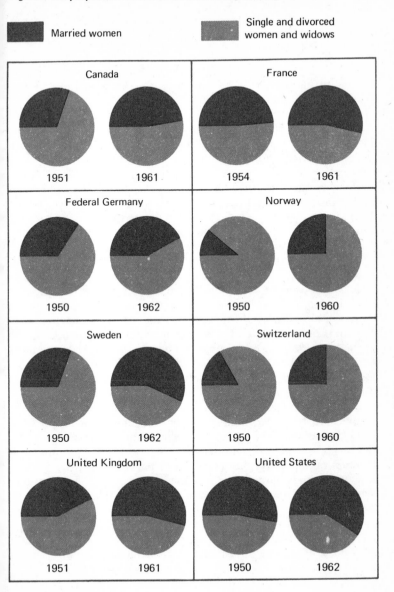

on a farm, in a shop or in a family firm. Most of these women worked throughout their adult life.

In modern times, and certainly since about 1950, the number of women at work is closely related to their age. The curve drawn by plotting female employment against age reaches its peak between twenty and twenty-four years of age. Leaving students aside, young women are nearly all employed at that time of their life. Between twenty-five and thirty-five the curve drops sharply, since this is the period of marriage and maternity. It rises again after thirty-five or forty depending on the country, attaining a second peak between forty-five and fifty. This bimodal distribution is changing somewhat. A remarkable increase is occurring in the number of women, generally married, who return to work when their children are grown up.

Thus the occupational life of western women is interrupted by marriage and maternity. Hence, promotion at work, even on a modest scale, is difficult for them. On the one hand, having interrupted their careers, they lose the advantages of seniority, the normal process by which employees proceed from grade to grade. On the other, they often have to face the difficulties of entering the labour market twice and thus compound the disadvantages due to discrimination against female workers, as well as other handicaps associated with each new start. In her first job, the young girl is assumed to be undependable, as she is eminently likely to drop work after a few years. Therefore, she is not given posts carrying responsibility and is considered a 'temporary'. This universal assumption has grave consequences in particular for the spinster who will never marry and yet who is treated as if she meant to leave her job on marriage. The labour market is thus biased against women from the start. Then again, when a married woman returns to work, she is rated as 'old' in a world where youth is considered synonymous with adaptability and resourcefulness. Age is a handicap which offsets the advantages of greater dependability. Unlike men, women have been shown to possess greater qualities of endurance and competence at forty than at twenty. However, since the labour market is ruled by men, it is dominated by male prejudices which may be justified in relation to male workers, but do not make sense when applied to women, as they regrettably tend to be.

When women resume work after a long break, it is like leaving one world to enter another. Our societies do very little or nothing at all to make this easier, despite the fact that we live in an age in which permanent retraining has become a necessity. The uncoordinated endeavours of various private undertakings and of several governments to facilitate re-entry into occupational life are small in relation to the needs. The right to work, inscribed in many national constitutions, indeed operates against heavy odds. Sweden undoubtedly stands out for her vigorous and intelligent efforts to facilitate this second entry into active life. However, we shall not be able to assess the results of her policy until 1980.

Moreover, many women find it impossible to resume their earlier trade when entering the labour market for the second time. This is particularly true of jobs requiring youthful attractiveness; it applies not only to the obvious cases of models or cover girls, but also to many secretaries and salesgirls. Women of over thirty-five are rejected because the secretary or salesgirl is expected to project a sexual image as well as to do her job. Nothing substantiates this point better than a glance at the 'Situations Vacant' column which repeats the phrase 'A young woman between twenty and thirty years of age' like a litany.

These demands will only diminish when the need for labour increases. Thus in the United States the manpower shortage created by the war, in conjunction with Federal Government pressures, was needed to force employers to accept women over thirty-five. Nowadays they have shown themselves equal to the task and the need for labour continues at a high level. Nevertheless, unemployment or under-employment affects older women before the younger ones. For example in Italy it is extremely difficult for women to return to work when their children are grown up, because of the permanent under-employment of female workers.

Table 3:2 Increase in the percentage of American women working, classified by age groups, during the period 1940-65

Age groups	In relation to total population	In relation to the labour force
14-19 years	36·7	68·7
20-24	14·1	16·1
25-34	4·5	12·4
35-44	36·4	117·0
45-54	49·7	207·8
55-64	70·2	292·1
65 and over	116·0	230·3

Figure 6 Increasing percentage of working women over 45 in the USA

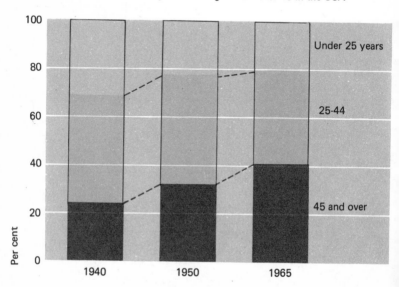

The moment a married woman leaves her job, there are younger ones to replace her.

The increasing average age of working women
This is the most striking result of recent evolution. When people are asked to guess the average age of working women, their answers bear no relation to reality, since they imagine as typical the twenty-five year old. In fact the average greatly surpasses this everywhere, although perhaps the United States holds the record with its average of forty-two years old. Of course for such an average to exist there must be many women workers over forty-two, and this implies that many of over fifty-five or even sixty are still employed. But public opinion does not notice them in its concentration on the youthful image which epitomises the female sex. The same trend prevails in Canada, as one can see by figure 7.

The situation is similar in Denmark where the highest rate of female employment is recorded between the ages of thirty-five and fifty-five.

In France – and to a certain extent in Germany and Austria – women employed in agriculture, a way of life widely different from that of other occupational categories, should be considered separately. Table 3:5 shows the rate of employment of French women in non-agricultural occupations since 1906. As indicated in the table, there has been a decrease in the proportion of young women under twenty who work, due to the increase in education. The rate of employment has increased between the ages of twenty and twenty-four, while for the age group twenty-five to forty little change has been registered from the beginning of the century. Since about 1950 the proportion of working women over forty has grown and the increase is nearly ten per cent for the age group fifty to sixty. Since pensions are widespread, employment decreases after sixty-five, contrary to the pattern prevailing in the United States. Even in Spain, where the situation is so different, a slight movement in this direction has been recorded in recent years (see table 3:4) After forty women tend to work more than they did

Figure 7 Percentage of working women in Canada according to age

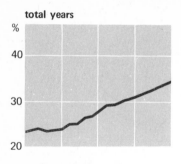

total years
%
40
30
20
1950   55   60   65   70

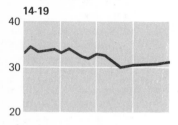

14-19
40
30
20
1950   55   60   65   70

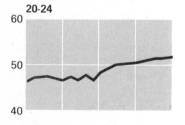

20-24
60
50
40
1950   55   60   65   70

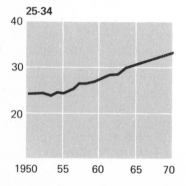

25-34
40
30
20
1950   55   60   65   70

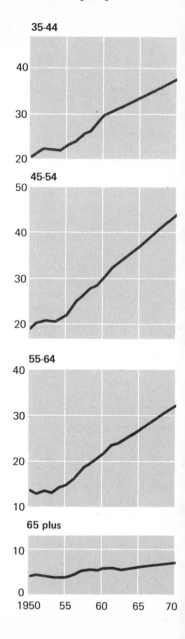

35-44
40
30
20
1950   55   60   65   70

45-54
50
40
30
20
1950   55   60   65   70

55-64
40
30
20
10
1950   55   60   65   70

65 plus
10
0
1950   55   60   65   70

Table 3:3 Danish women working as percentage of age groups, 1966

15-19 years	37
20-24	48
25-34	46
35-44	53
45-54	54
55-64	36
65 and over	10

Table 3:4 Percentage of Spanish women working in 1966

20 to 24 years	45·1
25 to 29	28·2
30 to 35	20·9
40 to 59	23·0

Table 3:5 Percentage of French women working (excluding agriculture), classified by age group

Age group	1906	1936	1946	1962
15-19 years	42·7	39·3	36·5	37·4
20-24	40·5	39·0	39·5	50·6
25-29	33·5	31·7	33·2	35·8
30-34	30·5	28·9	30·2	31·4
35-39	29·8	28·8	29·9	31·8
40-44	28·8	29·1	30·1	33·5
45-49	27·2	27·9	30·1	35·5
50-54	25·0	24·9	28·7	34·1
55-59	21·1	21·2	24·7	30·7
60-64	18·6	16·8	19·4	22·7
65-69	15·3	12·8	12·6	11·0

between the ages of thirty and thirty-five. This trend is more pronounced if the 872,000 Spanish women working in agriculture are not taken into account.

The only exception to this modern trend is Holland, which has always been a 'deviant' case. The number of women working has decreased between 1947 and 1960 (both in absolute numbers and as a percentage) and the rate of employment of women over forty-five has also declined from 16·9 to 13·4 per cent. The only age group in which this rate has advanced is that of young women aged between fourteen and nineteen years, for which it is very high and has passed from 48·7 to 49·8 per cent.

Continuous employment versus interrupted employment

This chapter would not be complete without noting that these patterns do not characterise the People's Democracies. There women often study for long periods of time, and they bring up their children, but they do not stop working for these purposes. They have one advantage over men, which is that they can retire earlier, either at fifty-five, or at fifty in some cases, or even earlier if they have a large family. This constitutes a totally different pattern of life for women – their careers are uninterrupted, which perhaps in itself serves to explain why so many attain professional success. On the other hand, the years of motherhood are hard, despite all leaves of absence and special provisions like nurseries and summer camps. In observing everyday life in the Soviet Union, one is struck by the small size of families and by the extent to which children are spoilt, particularly by their grandmothers. With early retirement at fifty or fifty-five, these still vigorous women generally put themselves at the service of their daughters and daughters-in-law. It should also be noted that the working day is shorter than in the West and that pressures for high output in offices and factories have decreased. In spite of all this, women make great efforts to gain the maximum amount of leave for maternity, illness and holidays, often being away from work for six months or even a whole year when they are having children, safe in the assurance

From Yugoslavia an age-old solution: grandmother watches the baby while the mother works. This still happens in Russia today, but is becoming uncommon in western countries.

Left A nursery in a Murmansk village, USSR. Russia and the countries of eastern Europe provide numerous children's nurseries so that the mothers can work. In the West, by contrast, there is approximately one nursery for every 125,000 inhabitants. *Below* Women on strike at the Herstal arms factory (see page 128) demand nurseries for their children.

that they will not lose their jobs. In this context reactions to a proposal for female retirement at fifty showed that many unions of women workers preferred the existing norm of retirement at fifty-five, if these additional five years could be given as leave during the period of child bearing and child rearing.

There is a movement in the People's Democracies even more than in the Soviet Union in favour of the years of motherhood being spent in the home, while paradoxically in the West many women's associations demand the provision of additional nurseries and kindergartens.

This shows the complexity of the problem. How can justice in promotion in an occupational structure dominated by men be reconciled with women's reproductive role, which makes their lives discontinuous by definition? It seems that the working mother suffers more than her children, despite all that has been said on the subject. The children of working mothers do not have higher rates of sickness, or lower rates of development, they are no worse adjusted (on the contrary they compare favourably) and no more delinquent, despite the tissue of lies that one reads, than the children of mothers who remain in the home. On many of these

After looking after their children for
a few years, many women now take
retraining courses, as here in Paris,
and return to work.

107

points one can even cite evidence to show that children of working mothers do better than those of non-working mothers, although a copious literature seeks, without any substantiation, to designate such children as martyrs. However, the women themselves, if they continue work, find life infinitely more difficult, at least for a few years.

The other side of the coin is the number of difficulties to be negotiated if the mother does stop work and then finds herself at forty, lonely, without enough to fill her time, in a house which is often empty. All doctors confirm that such women have a greater tendency towards nervous complaints than their counterparts who work. Nor do they have an easy time of it if they seek to re-enter the labour market and are immediately faced with a choice between being retrained or accepting an uninteresting and monotonous task, well below the level they could have reached, had their working life been uninterrupted. This is not a very promising picture and it becomes even more depressing if one considers the wages paid to millions of working women.

4 The economics of employment

It is in those countries which have registered the greatest economic prosperity over the last twenty years that the number of women working appears to have increased most. Hence the employment of women seems to be an index of prosperity rather than one of decline.

In countries such as the United States or Canada the rate of female employment before the Second World War was extremely low, and inferior to that observed in most of Europe during the same period. This was certainly due to the large contingent of adult men of working age who arrived as immigrants to America. Since the end of the war the number of women at work in these countries has increased so rapidly that it has doubled in fifteen years and continues to mount. This development has been accompanied by an unprecedented prosperity. Affluence stimulates consumption, which in turn stimulates production, and both have the joint effect of creating jobs. The same phenomenon occurred in Sweden and even in Germany where the rate of female employment was already high. The modern affluent society thus appears to increase employment prospects for women and facilitate their integration into economic life, a development which is more difficult during periods of recession and unemployment.

Contrary to nineteenth-century beliefs which have left such a residue in modern thought, low rates of female employment do not presage well for a society. They do not indicate that men are earning so well that women have no need to work. In Belgium for example it was the economic stagnation of the coalmining areas whose population is French-speaking which accounts for the fact that so few women work, whereas the prosperity of the Flemish regions results in greater female employment. However, this law should not be interpreted as holding under all conditions. The Netherlands, for instance, tend to be an exception, being very prosperous and yet registering a low (although increasing) rate of female employment. While the overall figures of working women in Italy, Austria and France have if anything declined, this is due to special conditions and does not invalidate the general rule.

Fiction and reality

Before we look at the statistical data on this problem, we must note that within any one society the ideal role assigned to women may be strikingly different from their actual position with regard to employment. The following examples show the extent of this disparity.

The proportion of women who work is almost identical in Spain and the Netherlands (23 per cent and 22 per cent respectively), while it is considerably higher in, for instance, Federal Germany (37 per cent), Great Britain and France (both about 34 per cent). However, it does not follow that the general conception of woman's social role as held by public opinion is the same in Spain as in the Netherlands. This is far from being the case. The Netherlands enjoys a democracy permitting the kind of debate on sexual freedom, contraception and female emancipation which could never take place in Spain, at least not with the same openness and outspokenness. Indeed Spanish women do not fully come of age legally until twenty-five – a provision which would scandalise Dutch girls. Yet the two countries have almost the same proportion of working women, and Spain even leads by a short head. Thus there is no connexion between the prevailing view of women's role and the part which they actually play in production, between principles and practice. Principles are inherited from the past, while practice is governed by the economic needs and demographic factors of the present.

Everyone has heard the German slogan 'Kinder, Küche, Kirche' ('children, kitchen, church') which consigned the German or the Austrian woman to the duties of the home. Nevertheless, in Germany and in Austria (in spite of the prevalence of Catholicism) the highest rates of female employment in the western world, Finland excepted, have long been recorded.

Female employment is high in Catholic Italy, which has always endorsed a very tranditionalist view of women's home role, originating from both Latin and Catholic philosophy. Thus the famous Papal Encyclicals *Casti Connubi* and *Quadragesimo Anno*, which amplified the doctrine laid down in *Rerum Novarum*, both condemned women's pursuit of earnings outside the home. Nevertheless, both Italy and France – another Latin and Catholic country – have known high rates of female employment, which for a long time have been double that of the United States, despite the latter's more modern view of women's independence and equality with men. To take up the example of Belgium again: today for every hundred men there are forty-eight women in employment in the Flemish-speaking regions whereas in the French-speaking area of Charleroi there are only twenty-one and in the neighbourhood of Huy the ratio drops to nineteen. Yet women at work are condemned on religious grounds among the Catholic Flemish population, while it is the more tolerant French-speaking Belgians that register the lowest rates of female employment for the whole of Europe.

Therefore it seems clear that the prevailing ideology is insufficient to explain differences in rates of employment that often run counter to the dominant social norms and reflect economic or demographic pressures.

The difficulty of international comparisons

Three types of statistical data may give an idea of the relative importance of female employment:

1 The absolute number of women working at a given date in the country considered.

2 The proportion, expressed as a percentage, of working women in relation to the total number of women.

3 The proportion, expressed as a percentage, of working women in relation to all workers of both sexes.

However, it is difficult to compare two countries by consulting these data, since such indices do not necessarily follow the same criteria. For instance, in some countries women working part-time are counted among the active population, even if they only work several hours a day or several months a year. This is the case in the United States where part-time work is widespread, above all among women. According to surveys conducted by the Bureau of Labor in 1964 and published at a later date, sixty-six per cent of the men who claimed to have worked in 1964 were in full-time employment throughout the year, whereas this was the case for only thirty-seven per cent of the women. On the other hand, out of a hundred women employed during that year, sixty-three had not worked full-time throughout, but:

either had worked shorter hours all year, at most thirty-five hours a week (nine);

or had worked full-time but not all year (fifteen had worked between twenty-seven and forty-nine weeks and sixteen between one and twenty-six weeks);

or had worked part-time for only part of the year (twenty-three).

In other countries, such as France, it is only women working full-time throughout the year who count as part of the active population. Part-time female workers 'are not covered by any official statistics because, for reasons connected more or less directly with taxation' (i.e. in order to retain the special allowance for families with one wage-earner only) 'they very rarely declare that they are employed'. This example illustrates the difficulty of comparing national statistics compiled on different bases.

Another difficulty facing the statistician and leading to variations in the coverage of female employment is the case of women working within the family enterprise. The wife or daughter of a farmer or a poulterer, a hotel keeper or a shopkeeper often works on the family land or in the family firm without receiving a fixed salary. Often her hours of work will be variable, some women slaving sixty hours a week, while others only give a hand for several hours each day. Whether or not the statistician includes this category in the active population may significantly increase or decrease the final rate of female employment. Thus as calculated from official statistics the percentage of women working in Italy has decreased between 1901 and 1936 from 32·4 to 24 per cent. Yet this statistical variation does not reflect a genuine change. During this period considerable efforts were made to give land to peasants and the number of

The proportion of women in agriculture
varies, according to the country,
from five to seventy per cent.

smallholders increased accordingly. Therefore women who as agricultural labourers were counted among the active population were subsequently registered in the census as housewives (*casalinga*) when their husbands acquired land. It seems likely that they worked just as hard, if not harder, than they had done as hired labour before the reform. Many such instances could be mentioned. Sometimes a single country can change its statistical definitions from one census to another, either including or excluding women who help on family enterprises. Thus in France, definitions have been more and more restrictive, so that fewer women in this category are counted among the active population.

Denmark, Luxemburg, Great Britain and the Netherlands do not include this group within their employment statistics. However, in these countries there are few women still engaged in agriculture, which is the sector of the economy traditionally most reliant on unpaid help within the family. On the other hand, in Austria, the Federal Republic, Italy, Portugal and Yugoslavia, a good proportion of the working women registered by the census belong to the latter category. In Austria they account for 24·2 per cent of the total number of women workers enumerated, in Italy – 24·3 per cent, in Yugoslavia – 25·7 per cent, in Portugal – 28·2 per cent and in the Federal Republic – 22·3 per cent.

The basis of employment statistics must also be taken into account. Generally such data are derived from the census, but in some countries this only takes place every ten years – and interim surveys conducted on sample populations are used to assess fluctuations in employment. Thus, in the United States, surveys take place every month utilising a sample of 35,000 households. From this one can either count all the women who worked in the course of one year, or calculate the average number of women workers. Since many women are employed on a seasonal or occasional basis, these two approaches yield very different results. For example, in 1964 33·1 million women were listed who had worked at one time or another during the year, whereas the average number of women in employment only reached 25·8 million, i.e.

Table 4:1 Working women as a percentage of total active population in each country (dates at which these figures were provided vary between 1963 and 1967).

USSR	48·0	USA†	34·1
East Germany	46·0	Yugoslavia	33·4
Poland	45·0	Greece	32·8
Czechoslovakia	43·0	Belgium	31·6
Finland	43·0	Switzerland	30·1
Austria	41·3	Italy	29·0
Turkey	40·9	Canada*	27·1
Federal Germany*	36·9	Eire	26·7
Sweden†	36·5	Spain	23·0
Denmark†	35·3	Netherlands	22·9
France	34·9	Norway	22·9
Great Britain*	34·4	Luxemburg	20·0
		Portugal	18·4

In countries marked with an asterisk part-time women workers account for at least ten per cent of working women, whereas they account for over twenty per cent in countries marked with a dagger.

a difference of 7·3 million. Both figures have been obtained from representative samples of respondents and not, as in most other countries, from a general census.

Attention should also be paid to the basis upon which percentages of female workers are calculated. In some countries they are given as a proportion of active women to total female population, while in others, mainly in eastern Europe, they are usually calculated on the basis of the female population between fifteen and sixty years of age. This difference of approach is not always made clear and obviously produces dissimilar results.

Female employment as a percentage of total employment of both sexes appears to provide the most useful data. It gives good indication of sex differences in employment and also of the relative importance of women's contribution to the economy. It is, however, indispensible to relate this percentage to the structure of the given population. Thus when it is stated that out of every hundred Soviet workers forty-eight are women, in other words, that one

Below Women in the cotton fields of
Anatolia, Turkey, and *right* a woman
in a cement factory in East Germany.
Stereotyped ideas of femininity
must sometimes go by the board.

worker in two is female, one must bear in mind the enormous surplus of women of working age within the adult population of the Soviet Union.

Since further comments on the unreliability of female employment statistics would make tiresome reading, let it suffice to stress the difficulty of international comparisons. Indeed, a standardisation of basic definitions such as that of working women, of part-time employment, etc., would be of benefit to all, and to sociologists in particular. Within the limits of one country, historical comparisons yield more precise results provided that the classification of women helping in the family enterprise does not change from year to year.

In the People's Democracies, including Yugoslavia, the weekly hours of work are shorter than in the West – forty to forty-two hours and sometimes less, as against forty-five to forty-eight in the majority of western countries, except Canada, France and Belgium which have established the forty-hour week, and the United States which is moving in this direction.

The considerable variation in rates of female employment from country to country reflects their historical differences.

Countries with increasing female employment

In this group of countries, female employment has sharply increased since the last war. They include the United States, Sweden and the People's Democracies, as well as Yugoslavia.

In the specific case of the People's Democracies political change resulted in the increased number of women at work. However, before the war in largely rural countries such as Romania, Poland, Hungary, Bulgaria and Yugoslavia, the women who worked in agriculture were not always enumerated as active population by the census, as they are today. In some of these countries the rural population represented sixty to eighty per cent of the total population, and the women of this group were certainly not inactive.

The case of the United States and of Sweden is quite different, since before the war they were economically advanced, but the

proportion of women working was particularly low. In this connexion it is paradoxical that Betty Friedan should look back
nostalgically to the 'thirties which were, according to her, the years
of female activity and initiative, in contrast to today's herd of
consumers manipulated by hidden persuaders. In fact the ratio of
working women to housewives in 1930 was half that recorded
today in the United States. This rapid increase has been most
marked since 1960 – and in 1970 forty per cent of women work
(either part-time or full-time) as against twenty per cent in the
'thirties. This represents a revolutionary change in social norms.
Canada has lagged a little behind the United States, but if her rate
of female employment has remained very low for a long time it is
increasing even faster at present.

Countries with stable or decreasing female employment
In a second group of countries, female employment is a long
established tradition and has not changed appreciably as a proportion of the labour force. Only a slight increase has been recorded
since 1960 in Great Britain and in Denmark. In fact there were
more Danish working women in 1911 in relation to the total
population than there are now. A similar trend prevails in Germany
where there is a long history of female employment. In the twentieth
century, however, political factors influenced employment rates;
Hitler intended to reduce the number of working women, above
all in the jobs carrying prestige, but was forced by the war to rely
upon their services in factories, offices and hospitals. In the post-
war period the employment of women increased considerably, but
did not yet equal the rate of the early twentieth century (thirty-nine
per cent). Finland has both a high rate and a long record of female
employment. There is thus a great difference between Norway, on
the one hand, and Denmark, Sweden and Finland on the other,
all of which are characterised by high rates. This is one of the
disparities which should be remembered before indulging in
generalisations about Scandinavian women.
   A third group of countries can be distinguished in which the

proportion of working women has declined in relation to the level of employment maintained between 1900 and 1945. Thus in Norway at the beginning of the century women constituted 34·5 per cent of the active population while today they are only 22·9 per cent. Similar trends can be detected in Switzerland, Belgium and, above all, in France and Italy. One could add Austria to this category, even though she still heads western European records of female employment, as there has been a slight decrease since the early twentieth century (43·3 per cent of the active population, 47·4 per cent of female workers in relation to the total female population in 1900). In France the decrease has been from thirty-eight to 34·9 per cent and in Italy from 32·5 to 29 per cent.

As has already been discussed, the decline in employment rate in Belgium is due to regional causes affecting the French-speaking labour force. The reduction recorded in France and Italy can be attributed almost exclusively to the changes taking place in the agricultural sector of the economy. French agriculture now employs two million women *fewer* than it did at the beginning of the century. The Italian decrease has been equally marked and is not limited to agriculture, since industries such as textiles, where women workers used to be predominant, are increasingly replacing women by men. Both France and Italy still have a considerable rural population which should be reduced in the interests of the economy by alternative employment in the secondary or tertiary sectors. Women who worked on their husband's plot often cannot find re-employment on leaving the land, since the family home no longer coincides with the place of work. However, female employment in the tertiary sector (service activities, office jobs, professional posts) is steadily increasing in France and to a lesser extent in Italy, at a rate comparable with that of Anglo-Saxon and Scandinavian countries.

In dealing with developing countries one is struck by the inadequacy of statistical data on a problem as complex as that of female employment. The yearbooks compiled by the main international organisations quote very low rates of employment, but do

Girls cutting sugar cane in Brazil. They belong to the lowest social strata, the largely ignored *Lumpenproletariat*.

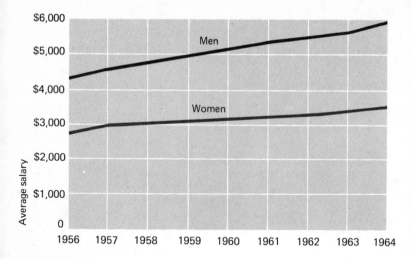

Figure 8 The increased earnings gap between men and women, 1956—64, in the USA

not indicate the sociological implications. They take no account of individual situations and apply the same rigid criteria to the female graduate training to be a journalist or a physician in Buenos Aires or Rio de Janeiro and to the peasant woman who grows her own food, such as it is, milks her goat, weaves her cloth, raises animals, makes her own utensils out of clay and wood. The former is working, whereas the latter is 'idle' according to statistical evidence. Therefore, it is vain to try and express in quantitative terms realities separated by such qualitative differences. Africa, Asia and South America elude attempts to provide a measure of women's contribution to the production and the life of their country. But although their share cannot be calculated, they are certainly far from being unproductive.

Wage discrepancies between men and women

So far we have kept to the hypothesis that the distance which has always existed between the position of men and that of women still exists in modern society. Let us put it to the test by considering economic factors. Many people believe that women have cause to be content with their present economic status.

Those who know classical literature are aware that there have been rich women in ancient societies and that poor men would stop at nothing in order to marry them. There is a whole anthology to illustrate this situation from Plautus to Balzac. Nowadays, fewer young men look for an heiress and marriage to provide them with a steady income. Nearly everyone lives on an income derived from work. This is not at all to women's advantage. Either they do not work and are economically dependent on their husbands, or they are under-paid in relation to male workers. In eighteenth-century society, for example, the caprice of fate, while it was 'socially' unfair, did not favour men financially rather than women. Of course, the women who had to earn a living were under-paid and remained so throughout the nineteenth century. The great gap between the wages of male and female operatives has not vanished, although it has shrunk for most trades. It still exists and seems likely to last. Thus in the United States the great distinction between wages paid to men and to women is *increasing*, albeit slightly, year after year (see figure 8).

The earnings of female clerical workers which in 1956 equalled seventy-two per cent of their male counterparts' income fell to sixty-six per cent in 1964. During the same period the wage ratio of women working in factories dropped from sixty-two to fifty-eight and that of salesgirls from forty-five per cent to forty per cent. In other words, the same shop will pay male sales staff twice as much as women doing exactly the same job. The salaries of female managerial and supervisory staff declined from sixty-four per cent to fifty-six per cent of the remuneration given to men in the same posts. Women technicians are now paid sixty-four per cent of the salaries granted to men, after having reached a peak of sixty-eight per cent in 1961. In service activities (other than domestic service) the ratio has declined from fifty-nine per cent to fifty-four per cent of men's wages. (See Handbook of Women Workers, US Department of Labor.) While these discrepancies are related to training or educational attainment, they cannot be fully explained by such considerations, since white American women who are generally better educated than coloured men (two more years schooling on average), are less well paid than the latter.

The level of female remuneration throughout the world is depressingly low. During the events of May 1968, French trade unions demanded an increase in the lowest rates and obtained some reforms. It was realised then that hundreds of thousands of people earned less than six hundred francs (approximately fifty pounds) a month. Many argued indignantly that it was impossible to live decently on such an income – and they were quite right. But they generally failed to note that seventy-five per cent of this *Lumpenproletariat* was composed of women.

Table 4:2 shows the difference between male and female earnings in France in 1964, and table 4:3 shows the average weekly wage, according to the Annual Abstract for 1967, of British manual workers in the same year. This table shows a difference of nearly fifty per cent. On the other hand, the weekly wage of administrative, technical and clerical employees in 1966 was £26.13.9 for men and £14.4.11 for women.

In Sweden, female clerical workers earned sixty per cent of the men's wage in 1950. After ten years the difference in gross earnings has slightly declined although the actual income of men has increased more than that of women (see table 4:4).

A study conducted by the Canadian Federal Statistical Bureau in 1968 revealed that the average remuneration of women workers was half of that paid to men in the same jobs, in spite of the rapid increase in the rate of female employment and of the greater variety of occupations open to women.

Nevertheless, a slight improvement has occurred in the West German wage structure. If the level of wages in 1958 is considered as base 100, the remuneration of male workers in 1964 equalled 164 and that of female workers 176.

In Denmark and in the Netherlands, differentials in wages (slightly decreased in Denmark since that country ratified ILO Convention 100 in 1961) are aggravated by heavy fiscal penalties for married women who work. If their husbands make a good living they may have to give up one-third of their own earnings to the Inland Revenue. It should be noted however that Dutch working wives contribute less to the family budgets than do their counterparts in other countries. A publication of Dutch Women's Associations states that wives contribute on average twenty per cent of the family income – a percentage so low as to be almost unbelievable. Yet official documents seem to confirm this surprising assertion.

Equal pay for equal work
It is difficult to ascertain to what extent this deplorable situation reflects the inadequacy of training and vocational guidance for women, as well as the unfavourable repercussions of their domestic responsibilities on their work (in, for example, absenteeism, shorter hours, interrupted activities). On the other hand sheer prejudice against women often undoubtedly results in lower pay for equal work without any justification, simply because they are not men: differences and unfair differentiation are so inextricably linked that they seem impossible to disentangle. This became obvious when the ILO and the European Community successively asked their members to sign provisions on equal pay for equal work (namely Convention 100 and for the Common Market countries Article 119 of the Rome Treaty).

The states which actually signed these international agreements did make considerable progress in this respect. However, differential levels of remuneration for female workers have too often been camouflaged by reclassifying jobs. The tasks performed by women merely have to be given a lower rating for their wages to remain unchanged. This can be illustrated by a recent example from the French printing industry. Modern linotypes are no longer controlled by compositors, but by a punched tape. These tapes are generally punched by female typists because it is quicker to train them to do this job than to teach it to male machine compositors. After two months' training women acquire a speed of 15,000 touches per hour, whereas after six months the men's score is

Table 4:2 Average remuneration of women in France as a percentage of average remuneration of men

Higher managerial workers	63
Medium grade managerial workers	68
Clerical workers	76
Manual workers	69

Table 4:3 The average weekly wage of British manual workers in 1964

Men	£20.1.7	Boys	£9.13.0
Women	£10.1.0	Girls	£6.15.3

Table 4:4 Monthly earnings of employees in Sweden

Year	Men	Women
1950	527 crowns	375
1955	772	531
1960	1,126	732
Hourly rates in industry		
1950	2·73	1·92
1960	6·82	4·71

Table 4:5 Gross weekly wages in industry in Federal Germany

Years	Men	Women
1964	186 DM	115
1966	216	137
Average monthly earnings of clerical workers		
1964	969	578
1966	1,134	690

Women begin to demand their rights.
A demonstration for equal pay in
the successful Herstal strike.

only 10,000. Yet in spite of their higher output women are paid at the typists' rate (800 francs per month), while men get the compositors' rate (1,500 francs per month). In the records of the firm the one is called a typist and the other a compositor, although they use the same machine. The most efficient women workers get only fifty-five per cent of the remuneration given to the least efficient men, but this discrimination is hidden by the different names given to their respective jobs.

It is general practice in job classification to overrate physical strength and underrate dexterity, even for tasks requiring no use of strength. Trade unions, largely made up of men and under male leadership, often make no criticism of this form of discrimination. The strike of women workers at the Herstal arms factory in Belgium in 1966 was necessary to rally public opinion against this malpractice concealed by cant and bureaucracy. The four thousand women strikers at Herstal stayed out for three months until the principle of equal pay for equal work was recognised in their factory. Previously, a skilled operative (female) tending three machines earned less than the yard-sweeper and the messenger boy. This strike drew the attention and support of women throughout Europe, initiating a great movement of female solidarity. Rarely has one seen a strike conducted with more determination and winning more popularity.

The present situation
At the moment each member state of the European Community is endeavouring to fulfil its obligations in this respect, but the adjustment of women's wages is taking place very slowly. Delaying tactics, passive resistance and endless stalling interrupt its progress Ten years after signing the Treaty of Rome, on 31 July 1967 the Commission of Social Affairs of the EEC voted a draft resolution stating that:

The provisions required to ensure the full implementation of the principle of equal pay have not yet been taken in all member states.

GA.....LISATION DES SALAIRES

ÉGALITÉ

The procedures guaranteeing that courts of law will uphold this principle have not been instituted in all member states.

One member state has not yet ratified ILO Convention 100. This is despite the fact that on 31 December 1961 the member states had committed themselves to 'completely eliminating all forms of discrimination before 31 December 1964'.

In 1968, the situation prevailing in member countries of the Community was largely as follows:

In Belgium the growth of wages paid to women has been much faster than that of men's wages (a difference of twenty-two per cent which is indicative of the size of the gap to be closed).

In Germany the Federation of Employers stated that the principle was now fully implemented in practice. However, the Federation of Trade Unions (DGB) rejected this opinion, pointing out the continued existence of special rates for certain jobs labelled 'light work' which are exclusively feminine, and quoting many collective agreements which imply discrimination against women.

In France one finds the same type of disagreement as in Germany, this time between the government which declared its satisfaction with the present situation and the unions who accepted the general classification of jobs as fair, but maintained that some discrimination prevailed in relation to certain tasks performed by women.

In Italy, court jurisdiction in this respect is contradictory. The government stated that it could not impose equal pay as a condition for the validity of collective agreements. In the industries in which unionisation is weak, the principle of equal remuneration goes unrecognised. Yet the principle of women's right to equal pay is incorporated in Italian legislation.

In the Netherlands the situation is very unfavourable to women as the government tends to hide behind statements that 'the present economic situation requires great prudence', although minimum wages have lately been increased. The Commission of Social Affairs of the EEC made the following critical comment: 'We are compelled to state that the Netherlands figures among those states which have only extended the principle of equal pay to those jobs undertaken by both sexes', while tasks mainly performed by women continued to be underpaid. 'Moreover, it is regrettable that the Netherlands is the only country at present where female workers cannot improve their position by collective bargaining or similar procedures and yet are not protected by law against wage discrimination.'

In Great Britain, the only country which did not sign a single text guaranteeing equal pay for equal work, the situation is even worse. A typical example was provided by the Stockport factories of Roberts Arundel, where in 1966 fifty-one men earning twenty pounds a week were replaced by fifty-one women working the same machines for ten pounds a week. Female civil servants are paid the same as their male counterparts, and in the professions women are not expected to charge lower fees than men, and certainly not to undercut. It is in the private sector that there is most wage discrimination. Entry into the Common Market would involve large scale adjustments in wages, though the greater differentiation in Britain between jobs performed by men and by women (jobs done by both sexes being rare) would allow discrimination to continue against women. Some progress has been made, however, in mechanical engineering, the leather industry and the rag trade. Yet, according to Routh, the gap between ninety per cent of women's wages (apart from the top ten per cent of women wage earners) and the corresponding male wages was greater in 1959 than in 1911. Investigations commissioned by the Labour Party show that while 'more than a third of Britain's workers are women, it is estimated that only a tenth of these receive remuneration equal to that of men in the same position'. Government estimates of the cost of equalising remuneration were made in 1966 by the Ministry of Labour and placed the figure somewhere between 600 and 900 million pounds per year. Such equalisation would affect between three and seven million women, depending on the posts covered.

In the United States, while thirty-four states, the District of

Columbia and Puerto Rico have introduced minimum wage legislation this applies to both sexes only in twenty-two states and in Puerto Rico. In the remaining twelve states these laws apply only to women, while the other states have no legislation of this kind. The Federal Fair Labor Standards Act of 1938 established an hourly minimum wage rate for men and women. However, this Act does not apply to the retail trade and service activities, since federal jurisdiction does not cover hotels, motels, restaurants, laundries, shops or farming. Twenty-five states out of fifty have passed laws on equal pay which prohibit wage discrimination based on sex. Five other states also possess various forms of labour legislation which tend to the same end.

Nevertheless, the report of the Commission on the Status of Women founded by President Kennedy declared that:

Lower payment for women doing the same job as men is common. For example, studies carried out in 1960 have shown that the average female cashier with less than five years experience earns between five and fifteen dollars less per week than the average male cashier with the same experience; differences ranging between nine and forty-nine cents per hour have been found in the remuneration of men and women laundry-workers in several cities.

In February 1962, the Commission adopted the principle of equal pay, and an act implementing it and amending the Fair Labor Standards Act of 1938 was signed by President Kennedy in June 1963. Moreover, under Article 7 of the Civil Rights Act which came into force in July 1965, women can have recourse to federal arbitration in cases of discrimination. However this procedure is long and ponderous, and unknown to the majority of female workers. Despite this it is interesting to note that a third of the complaints lodged under Article 7 of this Act originate from women – the other two-thirds being made up of protests against racial discrimination. It can be hoped that this legislation will remedy a situation particularly unfavourable to women employed in the tertiary sector.

Canada, like the United States, has not ratified the ILO Convention 100. In 1956 the Federal Parliament passed a law on equal pay, but again as in the United States, it applied only to industries and activities of national rather than provincial importance. This leaves out the retail trade and the majority of service industries. Moreover, seven of the Canadian provinces have passed legislation on equal pay in the early 'fifties. Nevertheless, the studies conducted by Sylvia Ostry for the Bureau of Statistics using data from the 1961 census showed that in twenty per cent of cases, sexual discrimination operated which could not be explained away by reference to differences in qualifications, age, seniority or hours worked.

Since 1945 the employment of women has changed more than mere numbers alone can convey in that the type of work done by women and the categories of women who do the work have changed.

This evolution started during the 1914-18 war, but even at the beginning of the twentieth century women could be divided into two categories. The first consisted of those who were obliged to work in order to make a living, and who entered employment from the age of fourteen or fifteen or even earlier and continued in it to the end of their lives – unless they were lucky enough to marry 'well' so that they could leave their job. The second category of women never worked in their lives, in fact they considered 'woman' and 'work' to be incompatible terms. A 'real' woman, in other words one who came from a good family, did not work, and if forced by circumstances to do so, she felt degraded. The governesses and teachers who abound in novels of the time experienced the anguish of not knowing any longer where they belonged; they felt that they were not accepted in society because they had to earn a living.

After the First World War, this dichotomy broke down. In many countries, including England, the United States, Germany, France and Belgium, a redistribution occurred within the female population. The ranks of domestic servants, which had been so numerous in the past, were reduced by hundreds of thousands. Between June 1914 and June 1918 they shrank by 450,000 in Great Britain, 350,000 in the United States and 200,000 in Germany. With the end of the war women did not return to domestic service. Nor did many agricultural female workers return to the land, preferring to work in a factory. Both these groups chose a life in the workshop or factory which they found less arduous, restrictive and lonely. It is often alleged that women workers are undemanding and content with whatever conditions they find; their lack of protest is seen as an explanation of their subordinate occupational position. It is thus very important to underline the determination required to withdraw from domestic service in numbers and to stay away from it, resisting the temptation of wages often higher than those available in industry. The motto of the Austrian female strikers in the 'thirties was 'Anything rather than a return to bondage', as they steadily refused to become housemaids. The supply of servants in many countries has been abruptly and definitively cut off, not so much as a result of economic change as the reflection of a new outlook among women from the underprivileged classes. Spain and Portugal and, to a lesser extent, Italy have experienced a cultural lag in this respect, but are now catching up quickly. There seems to be a threshold at which the poorest women prefer their poverty to alienation and their independence to relative security. In 1931 domestic servants still represented 23·8 per cent of women working in Britain, while today they form less than 10 per

CRINOLINE FOR DOMESTIC USE.

Missus. "MARY! GO AND TAKE OFF THAT THING DIRECTLY! PRAY, ARE YOU AWARE WHAT A RIDICULOUS OBJECT YOU ARE?"

cent. In Austria during the same period the number of female servants declined from 158,000 to 45,000. However, the greatest change of all has been the growth (particularly in the 'fifties) of women's employment in the tertiary sector – secretaries, clerks, shop assistants, nurses, primary school teachers, etc.

The primary sector

The number of women employed in agriculture is decreasing steadily:

In France by 500,000 between 1954 and 1968, which represents a reduction of 29·3 per cent, whereas the male agricultural worker population dropped by only twenty per cent.

In Italy by 730,000, between 1961 and 1967, i.e., a decrease of 34·6 per cent for women, as against 22·5 per cent for men.

In Austria the decline is proportionally sharper though the absolute figures involved are smaller – in 1931 133,605 women worked in agriculture, in 1951 only 96,463 remained, and by 1961 this figure had been cut by half to 47,255.

In the United States this decline occurred much earlier and largely during the First World War.

The proportion of women in the agricultural sector of the economy still varies considerably from country to country. Table 5:1 gives an idea of the magnitude of these disparities. It is clear that Scandinavia and the English-speaking countries employ very few women in agriculture, while in central and eastern Europe the majority of agricultural workers is female. Latin and Mediterranean countries are mid-way between these extreme types. On the other hand, Finland is closer to the eastern Europe pattern than to the Scandinavian. The rate of female employment in the primary sector is very high in the Soviet Union, Poland, Romania and Bulgaria. Several factors should also be borne in mind in interpreting this table: first, one must mentally correct for the number of women working in family farms who are not counted in the active population in certain countries. Secondly, one must note

Table 5:1 Percentage of women employed in the primary sector and total labour force

Country		Primary sector	Total labour force
Canada	(1967)	11	30
USA	(1966)	18	35
Austria	(1961)	53	40
Belgium	(1966)	25	30
Denmark	(1967)	25	37
Eire	(1961)	11	26
Finland	(1960)	35	40
France	(1962)	33	33
Federal Germany	(1966)	54	36
Greece	(1961)	40	33
Italy	(1966)	31	27
Netherlands	(1960)	9	22
Norway	(1960)	5	23
Sweden	(1960)	9	30
United Kingdom	(1966)	11	32

differences in the years for which information is provided, many countries not having carried out a census since the early 'sixties, while for others the results of recent census data have not yet been published. In some cases considerable change has occurred in the interim period. Lastly, the United States and Canada provide data based on sample surveys rather than national census.

The secondary sector

The number of female workers in industry has remained stable or has slightly decreased in many countries. However, these variations are differently distributed throughout the sector. There are comparatively fewer trades and types of factories in which women are found. They are concentrated in specific lines of manufacture and in these are often in the majority. Generally they are unskilled or only semi-skilled and usually the wages in those concerns employing most women are lower than in branches where men predomi-

nate. The Soviet Union is exceptional in this respect, since many more jobs are filled by women in a wide variety of industries. Nevertheless even in the USSR female employment is concentrated in the most mechanised types of production. It can almost be stated as a general law for industry that women have one superiority over men – dexterity. Consequently many women are found in manufacturing industries requiring manipulation rather than strength. Women can attain a speed and accuracy of execution to which men cannot pretend. The pace of assembly lines on which women are employed can rarely be equalled by men.

However, this superiority of speed and dexterity is not acknowledged by commensurate wages. It is a fact that modern industry does not reward dexterity at its true worth. This is clearly a result of the ease with which female operatives can be found to perform jobs requiring speed and repetition, since unemployment is endemic among women. Consequently the wages paid for dexterity

A girl assembling electrical components.
Female dexterity (greater than male) is
rarely paid according to its true value.

remain low – unlike the constantly increasing remuneration given
for jobs requiring only strength, since men willing to undertake
unskilled manual labour are in short supply. Moreover, women
being less unionised have less influence on the development of
their wage structure which is not reassessed as often as in other
more organised types of employment.

Women in industry are mainly given jobs whose outstanding
characteristics are speed and monotony. One could perhaps add a
third factor: these tasks are sometimes the dirtiest and occasionally
are downright repellent, falling to women when they are rejected by
men (for example coring, scouring, polishing).

While the overall rate of female workers varies from country to
country, in general the majority of them is found in textile and
clothing manufacturing and in food processing industries. This
concentration is a hangover from earlier, pre-industrial times and
reflects the fact that clothing and cooking were traditionally female
activities. Yet female employment in the textile industry has been
decreasing steadily in almost all advanced industrial countries. In
the nineteenth century it was by far the greatest employer on the
market for men and women alike. It is not an accident that Marx
takes almost all his examples of current working conditions from
this particular industry. In the last few years modern equipment
has made it possible to dispense with the services of many female
workers. In a sense they have been superseded by male workers
possessing the high technical qualifications required in mechanised
factories and filling jobs for which women are not trained. Thus
female operatives remain predominantly semi-skilled or unskilled,
whereas it would have been comparatively easy to give them appropriate training and to find among them the staff capable of tending
new machinery. However, Britain is the only country to have
given women training. In other countries, such as Italy, the consequences on the female unemployment rate have been serious.
Between 1961 and 1967 female employment in Italian industry
decreased by 312,000, while male employment grew by 448,000.

While a marked decrease of female employment in the textile

industry has taken place in many countries, it has been compensated for by the proliferation of other jobs available to women, particularly in metallurgy and to an even greater extent in mechanical engineering, electricity and electronics. In Federal Germany female employment in the iron and metallurgical industries has grown by 162·3 per cent between 1950 and 1961; in France the number of women employed in metallurgy for the year 1962 was approximately 400,000, which represented an increase of 42·9 per cent in eight years; in Austria this increase equalled 64 per cent during the period 1951 to 1961. However, it is mainly in the manufacture of electrical components that women workers have found an outlet. Thus 612,700 were employed in this field in the United States in 1965, an increase of 82 per cent in relation to 1950 despite the overall decline of female employment in American industry. Great Britain registered a record number of 575,130 women employed in the electrical trades in 1967. France experienced growth of 73 per cent over eight years, a figure which will certainly be larger in the results of the last census yet to be published. In Germany this leap forward occurred earlier with an increase of 313 per cent between 1950 and 1961.

In spite of this redistribution, female workers are still concentrated in a fairly small number of industries, while others in which they could easily find suitable tasks do not employ them. Not only are they restricted to a few jobs in industry, they are also handicapped by their lack of qualifications. They can hardly be blamed for being unskilled, since they are for various reasons deprived of adequate training before entering the labour market. Nowhere have strong and thoroughgoing measures been taken to remedy this state of affairs. The technical complexity of production is rising and job requirements are changing accordingly. But it does not really matter to women whether they are setting up looms or placing filaments in transistors, since in either case they are untrained and unskilled and therefore everywhere condemned to the most monotonous and repetitive of tasks, those which are most exhausting to the nerves and the least well paid.

Table 5:2 Comparison of male and female workers in manufacturing industries according to level of training

	Skilled			Semi-skilled		Unskilled		Under 18	Total
	High	Medium	Low	High	Low	High	Low		
Male	116	159	167	192	136	99	75	56	1,000
Female	11	3	79	185	303	109	151	132	1,000

These categories correspond to the official classification of skills established by the French Ministry of Social Affairs.

In France in 1964 for each thousand employees in the manufacturing industries there were forty-nine executives of whom only four were women and eighty supervisors of whom only six were women. If one considers the largest category, that of the operatives as distinguished from executive and supervisory staff, the two sexes can be compared in terms of their relative degrees of skills (see table 5:2)

Thus out of every thousand male workers 442 are skilled, while the corresponding ratio is only ninety-three for every thousand female workers. On the other hand women are much more numerous in the semi-skilled and unskilled categories or among young workers of less than eighteen years of age. In addition, this situation is found even in industries like textiles and clothing, where women represent up to eighty per cent of the work force. Perhaps one might think that old habits still prevail in these traditional sectors which have always employed a majority of women and relied on male foremen. However, the same pattern of skills exists in the most modern electronics industry, where there are no more than seventy-three skilled workers out of one thousand women, whereas the ratio for men is 479 to 1,000.

The same situation prevails in Great Britain. In mechanical engineering and electronics there are 575,130 female workers as against 1,566,390 male, i.e. a ratio of one to three. However, their division according to skills is disproportionate: among skilled workers who represent 39·9 per cent of the total workforce, 37·6 per cent are male and 2·3 per cent are female. Women however,

Many men in the nineteenth century were appalled by the idea
of women working in offices (*right* an 1869 cartoon) but
a generation later saw their daughters working as typists
or secretaries (*below right* an office of 1903).

Table 5:3 Pattern of female employment in the USA

Type of work	Total number in 1940	per cent	In 1950	per cent	In 1965	per cent
White collar	5,380,000	45·0	8,858,000	51·6	14,066,000	57·1
Services	3,350,000	28·9	3,939,000	22·9	5,854,000	23·8
Blue collar	2,400,000	20·1	3,464,000	20·2	4,053,000	16·4

substantially outnumber men among the sixty-five per cent who
are semi-skilled (47·3 per cent as against 17·7 per cent). A similar
pattern characterises metalwork industries: among the 38·7 per
cent of skilled workers, 35·3 per cent are male and 3·4 per cent are
female, while among the seventy-four per cent who are semi-
skilled there are 24·9 per cent men and 49·1 per cent women.
(Source: Ministry of Labour Gazette, January 1967.) Again in
Denmark the same picture is found. In 1967 mechanical engineering
employed 116,700 skilled men and only 300 skilled women.

More encouraging patterns are hard to find. However, one can
pinpoint the textile industry in England which employs many
skilled women; in France they have made spectacular progress in
industrial design and in Germany great steps forward have been
made due to the multiplication of training programmes.

However, the addition of further statistical data from various
countries would merely result in stressing the subordinate position
of women in industry. This is so despite the fact that during the
two world wars women took responsibility for the most specialised
and difficult jobs and showed themselves well able to cope. As

CIVIL SERVICE.

"EMPLOYMENT" OF WOMEN?

President Kennedy declared on the foundation of the Commission on the Status of Women:

Each time a country has found itself in difficulty, it was women who performed its many tasks to perfection. However, as soon as peace was restored, they were treated as if they constituted a marginal group whose potential is not used as it should be.

In the USSR, on the other hand, women are not an unskilled and marginal labour force. While they are unevenly distributed among different branches of industry, they still represent an important proportion of skilled operatives.

The tertiary sector

The most outstanding feature of female employment since the end of the Second World War has everywhere been the striking increase of its importance in the tertiary sector, mainly in office work and in service activities. Table 5:3, for the United States, is

A secretary from Ouagadougou, capital
of the Upper Volta. The youth and
charm of the secretary have now become
an international phenomenon.

most telling in this respect. This table illustrates the extent of women's growing participation in the tertiary sector – not only have the absolute figures increased from five to fourteen million, but their importance in relation to male employment has augmented. Out of a hundred American women working, nearly sixty are in white collar jobs. In all countries the number of female employees in the tertiary sector has increased, even in Italy where female employment is declining. In Italy in 1967 this sector counted 42,000 women more than in 1961. Elsewhere the growth in this respect has been even more spectacular. In almost every country, particularly in the developed economies, women outnumber men in clerical posts.

Secretarial jobs have pride of place as 'the ideal work for a woman'. This is rather ironical if one remembers the resistance put up by male secretaries in the nineteenth century to the intrusion of women in offices. In this vein Alexandre Dumas, who held a secretarial post before becoming a playwright and popular novelist, solemnly assured women that 'if they put one foot inside an office, they would lose every vestige of femininity'. One hundred and thirty years later, one could compile a picturesque anthology eulogising this 'typically feminine occupation' and advising secretaries how to 'get on with their boss' or how to 'adapt to his temperament', be it nervous or phlegmatic, extrovert or introvert. By a subtle evolution, the secretary has come to be considered as the female partner in a working couple and she is taught to act as a woman should, adapting to, obeying and discreetly helping her boss, so that he shines while she practises self-effacement in the background.

This enormous source of employment, office work, does nothing for the status of women – again they find themselves occupying the most subordinate positions and the least skilled posts. Among public employees in Sweden, 73·4 per cent of women belong to the lowest categories (the levels rated one to nine), whereas seventy-three per cent of men occupy posts in the higher categories (the levels from ten to twenty-seven). The same situation is duplicated in German Public Administration (see table 5:4).

Table 5:4 Percentage of women in the German Civil Service according to class

Civil Servants		Clerks	
Class one	1·2	Class one	5·9
Class two	2·2	Class two	8·8
Class three	13·4	Class three	65·5
		Class four	77·1

Table 5:5 Percentage of women in the French Civil· Service according to class

Civil Service Class	1954	1962
A (equivalent of administrative class in Britain)	21	27
B (equivalent of executive class in Britain)	54	57
C (equivalent of lower grades of the executive class in Britain)	32	37
D (equivalent of clerical class in Britain)	39	63

In the French Civil Service, with its long tradition of female employment, women's situation is not only better, but has improved recently, since women have benefited to a greater extent from the higher appointments. However, the complementary increase in the percentage of women employed in the lowest category of the public service shows that they have been recruited mainly to the lower grades (see table 5:5).

In developed countries some services are virtually monopolised by women. For instance, telephone employees are eighty-two per cent female in Germany, ninety-five per cent in the United States, ninety-five per cent in France, and 96·5 per cent in Canada. Nevertheless the technical jobs in Posts and Telecommunications are still a masculine preserve and the qualifications required for

A telephone exchange in 1901.
Women have always been allowed a near-
monopoly of this branch of employment.

employment in this sphere are gained in schools reserved in most countries exclusively to men.

Public health is also a 'female benefice', since women make up ninety per cent of nurses in Germany, Austria, Great Britain, Denmark, Norway, Switzerland, Finland and Greece, while in other countries this percentage oscillates between ninety and seventy-five per cent.

Trade and retail sales are yet another female domain. However, there are interesting variations from country to country – Canada, the United States, Great Britain and Sweden register record numbers of sales girls, while in Mediterranean countries, such as Italy, Greece, Yugoslavia and Spain, these totals are lower. In the first group of countries the charm and youth of the shop-assistant is

A Russian doctor and nurse.
Eight doctors out of ten in
the USSR are women.

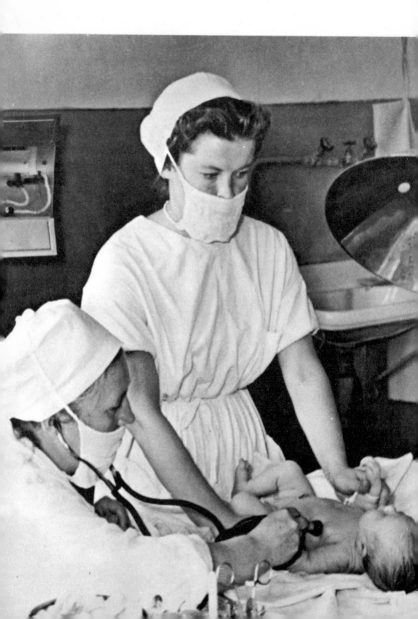

Table 5:6 Percentage of women in the medical profession

USSR	76
Great Britain	25
France	22
Federal Germany	20
Austria	18
Sweden	13
USA	6

almost a byword. In the latter, there is a kind of reticence about subjecting women and young girls to daily contact with the public. This difference in attitudes is reflected in services like hotels, restaurants and tourist bureaus – in Switzerland and Austria, it is women who predominate, whereas in Italy, so close geographically and so dependent on tourism, it is largely men who take this type of employment.

The professions

It is by examining women's position at the highest occupational levels that their changed status can be assessed. The professions, traditionally closed to female entrants, still represent the heights of prestige, authority, learning and income. Women's career prospects vary from country to country, although precise international comparisons are difficult to make. Attempts to investigate the numbers of women doctors, lawyers, engineers and teachers reveal great differences between countries. Without doubt the most striking example is that of the medical profession, as table 5:6

A woman sworn in as judge in Madagascar. Surprisingly enough for the conservative legal profession, women have found greater acceptance in law than in industry.

Table 5:7 Percentage of women barristers

USSR	38
France	19
Denmark	10
Austria	7
Sweden	6·7
Federal Germany	5
Great Britain	4 *
USA	3

* Data provided by the Central Office of Information. A survey of professional associations in 1964-5 revealed thirty-three women barristers out of a total of 283, i.e. 8·5 per cent.

Table 5:8 Percentage of women in the engineering profession

USSR	37
France	3·7
Federal Germany	1
USA	0·07
Great Britain	0·06

indicates. However, it is clear that the 360,000 women doctors in Russia do not have the same status as those in western Europe, let alone in the United States. Some of these included in the Russian figure will be officers of health rather than qualified physicians, their studies often being shorter than in the West. Even if one subtracts these partially qualified doctors, the Soviet Union counts

more women surgeons, specialists, hospital directors, than all western European countries put together. Not only is there a remarkably high percentage of women in the Soviet medical profession, there is also a high ratio of doctors to the population. On the other hand the pay for doctors is mediocre and the prestige no more than average if one compares it with western standards. By contrast the American doctor is really somebody in the community; he enjoys considerable pay and prestige. Women are virtually excluded from this highly rated profession – there are fewer female doctors in the USA than in Great Britain and the same number as in France whose population is four times smaller.

In Great Britain, in Germany and in France, it is the least remunerative sections of medicine in which the greatest concentration of women is found. They are clustered in the school medical services, the insurance companies, the social services and the more administrative posts for which men do not tend to compete. Thus even when the same initial training has been completed by both sexes, discrimination and differentiation occur within the profession itself and women are the losers in terms of pay and prestige.

There are also variations from country to country in the proportion of women in the legal profession, though these are less striking (see table 5:7). With the exception of eastern Europe, France and Finland, women judges and public prosecutors are extremely rare.

The difference between the USSR and western democracies is most marked in the membership of the engineering profession (see table 5:8).

The gap between 37 per cent in Russia and 3·7 per cent in France, the country with the next highest percentage, is staggering. Perhaps one might be tempted to think that the Soviet percentage only corresponds to a smaller number, but, on the contrary, this thirty-seven per cent of women engineers represents a contingent 500,000 strong. On the other hand, their French counterparts only number about 6,000, a figure which can just be doubled if one includes chemical engineers. Even if engineering degrees were

Table 5:9 Men and women in British engineering, 1965

Branch of engineering	Men	Women
Chemical	8,300	2
Civil	28,000	18
Mechanical	65,000	45
Electrical	56,000	116
Municipal	6,500	-

Table 5:10 Percentage of female staff in higher education in 1964 (or the year closest to it)

USSR	36	Finland	14
Romania	31	Austria	12
Poland	27	Sweden	11
Czechoslovakia	23	Greece	11
USA	22 *	Norway	8
France	20 †	Spain	7
Hungary	20	Federal Germany	6
Ireland	18	Italy	6
Great Britain	15	Netherlands	5
		Belgium	5

* Faculty board members only. The proportion in the United States has declined from twenty-six per cent in 1920, twenty-seven per cent in 1930 and twenty-eight per cent in 1940 to twenty-two per cent in 1965.
† Omitting teaching assistants.

easier to gain in the USSR, this difference remains in all its enormity and cannot be explained away by reference to total population size. The English-speaking, German and Scandinavian countries, famous for their advanced technology, only count an infinitesimal number of women engineers (figures taken from *Equality for Women*, Margherita Rendel, 1968, are shown in table 5:9). The percentage of female students at engineering schools and in universities granting diplomas in technology does not lead one to expect any leap forward. It is often said in the West that girls do not shine in mathematics. However, an annual selection procedure held in the Soviet Union to detect the most mathematically able pupils for training at Akademgorod, recruits an increasing number of girls each year – the present percentage is a good third of girls among the most gifted pupils.

To balance the negative picture of female prospects in western technology, the proportion of women pharmacists is more encouraging in Austria (51 per cent), France (42·2 per cent) and Federal Germany (40 per cent), although it is very low in other countries. Here and there women represent an important percentage of dentists: in France – 29 per cent, in Austria – 25 per cent, in Denmark 25 per cent, in Federal Germany – 25 per cent and in Sweden – 24 per cent.

The teaching profession is considerably more open to women, but here again female participation is greatest at the bottom of the pyramid. They are most numerous in primary teaching; almost everywhere they are in the majority (with the exception of Spain and Federal Germany) and in some countries elementary teaching is almost a female preserve (USA – 86 per cent, Great Britain – 80 per cent). At secondary level they are already less numerous. It is only in the USSR and in France that women outnumber men in secondary schools, being respectively 65 per cent and 51 per cent of the staff. Elsewhere they still constitute an important proportion of secondary teachers, for example 47 per cent in the USA, although in Mediterranean countries they are relatively less numerous.

However, at the top of the pyramid, in higher education, the number of women thins out (see table 5:10). The data are not strictly comparable as most of the countries listed include teaching assistants, whereas others restrict themselves to permanent staff.

Thus even in eastern Europe women are under-represented in higher education, though there are variations from country to country. The percentage of female academics is comparatively higher in underdeveloped countries.

Attitude to a professional career

It is extremely difficult to arrive at an overall assessment of women's progress in professional life. Only the USSR seems to give the picture of a country which has systematically opened careers to women, and its policy in this field seems to have been both consistent and successful. After the decimation of the male population during the Second World War, the contribution of a female élite was essential to Soviet society. One cannot help comparing the present situation with 1917 when only twelve per cent of Russian women were literate. (Certain other eastern European countries appear to have imitated this pattern.)

While France lags far behind the USSR in this respect, it does possess a female élite which is proportionally much greater than that of most western European countries. Since the last census of 1962, which is the source of the data given here, this trend has been magnified. It may be related to a historical tradition of female employment, to the organisation of higher education (open to women and non-fee-paying, though these characteristics exist in many other countries) and to a craving for equality between sexes stronger than in the English-speaking countries. Although their husbands do not help much in the home, except in the younger generation, French women lean towards feminism and seek an outlet in a career rather than in public or community life. Nevertheless, this important and competitive élite of professional women coexists in France with an exploited female proletariat at the bottom of the social ladder, in agriculture, industry and various service activities.

A New York teacher takes her pupils round a museum. School teaching is now largely in the hands of women.

American professional women are proportionally fewer, since working women are usually confined to very average jobs, which – because of the high level of remuneration in the United States – pay well enough. Thus career prospects are mediocre, a fact which always astonishes European girls travelling to America with the expectation of finding a country where women are at their most emancipated and independent. However, there is a great difference between personal freedom of behaviour for young women and their occupational opportunities. Young girls in England, Germany, America, Sweden, Denmark and Holland are more emancipated in their fashions, freedom to come and go, to travel alone and to date with boyfriends, than their Spanish, Italian and even French counterparts. On the other hand, the girl at a French university has no compunction about swotting in the hope of beating male students at their own game, while the American girl, according to Professor Mirra Komarovsky, 'tries to pass for more stupid than she is in order to please her boyfriend'. In her article in the *American Journal of Sociology*, she indicates that forty per cent of the girls interviewed admitted to having concealed some of their qualifications from their boyfriend. Also they were prone to give up arguments when they were about to win, deliberately lose at cards, make mistakes in their letters, and so on. This is a well-known attitude of 'pleasing by self-effacement' which for the young girl means presenting herself as less intelligent than she is, so as not to frighten men off.

Certainly French girls do this too, but not to the extent of concealing their qualifications in which, indeed, they generally take pride. In my own research I have not come across this 'fear of advancement for fear of the fear it would inspire in men' except among the most gifted and brilliant students who could pass any examination. When asked why so many of them entered for the '*agrégation*' (the very difficult competitive examination which leads only to teaching in French *lycées* or universities) instead of attempting the equally difficult entrance exam into the highest grade of the civil service, several answered that an administrative post carrying

authority and prestige would be a great impediment to finding a husband. By contrast, teaching also requires high qualifications at this level, but though respected as a career has neither sufficient prestige nor remuneration to frighten men away. All the same the degrees obtained were impressive ones and there was no question of concealing them on the marriage market.

Varying national attitudes
In view of the differences in female career prospects from country to country, it might be argued that the Protestant tradition in England and America has directed women towards voluntary work, in which their energy and talents are put at the disposal of the community often without remuneration, whereas French women seek an outlet in higher education and the professions. These historical differences of outlook and behaviour patterns

have done much to channel the activities of women along different lines. In France, 'charity' is unpopular with the younger generation of women who view the Lady Bountiful figure as outdated and insincere. By contrast, in the United States one can, according to a recent publication, even become a 'volunteer executive'. Nevertheless, in a society based on competition, the knowledge stakes, the diploma race and earning power, employment may be considered as the main criterion of social integration. Therefore the young housewife is wholly dependent on her husband whose financial and social success alone will enable her to be a respected and useful member of the community. This is an aspect of the American ideal of 'togetherness' which French women find both surprising and disturbing, despite the efforts of the mass media to popularise it. It is interesting to note in this connection that the studies carried out in France by the sociologist Chombart de Lauwe and his research team showed upper-class men to be the best disposed of all to the idea of women working.

The number of public statements made by American dignitaries, including the last two Presidents, supporting the advancement of women and lamenting their almost total absence from the professions, could make up a huge volume. In Great Britain, even with its tradition of Mrs Pankhurst and Dame Millicent Fawcett, their progress in professional life has only been slightly better. While women play an increasingly important role in British medicine, they are grossly under-represented in other careers of a comparable level. Various commentators have attributed this situation to deficient vocational guidance in schools and universities. Moreover, several sociologists allude to a prejudiced state of mind which can be illustrated clearly by a passage amusingly cited by Margherita Rendel from the *Radio Times* of 10 January 1966:

'X' earns about 9,000 pounds a year. . . . Attitudes have changed drastically over the last forty years in the civil service. Formerly, an elderly civil servant would shake with rage at the thought of having to put up with a Negro. But more recently one of the Under-Secretaries granted supreme recognition by saying: 'This is the mind of a White person'. 'Y' has reached the highest ranks of what was until now a White preserve: the diplomatic service. 'Y' distinguishes between the Black intellectual and the intelligent Blacks. 'It is hard for a Black to be an intellectual and to be unlike Whites, but an intelligent Black can easily remain very Black', according to him.

Margherita Rendel wonders whether such a text would not be construed as evidence of racial prejudice. Yet, in retelling the story, she has merely replaced the word 'Woman' by the word 'Black' and the word 'Man' by the word 'White'.

While English women retain their independence even after marriage, business matters tend to be discussed when the port is handed round in the absence of the ladies, or in a club from which wives, mothers and even mistresses are excluded. Over the Channel, where female company is inseparable from gracious living, men talk shop in front of women, who wait on their lords and masters, but join in the conversation. The idea of the male club has never taken root in France, despite endless attempts to establish it, while the notion of a ladies' club terrifies French women, who feel that they would be bored to distraction. At the same time it is in France that one finds the highest rate, eighty per cent, of women graduates who wish to continue working after marriage. And this does not remain in the realm of aspirations, but is reflected by facts; for France has the highest percentage of women graduates who continue to work after the age of twenty five (eighty per cent).

This is even more striking when one thinks that the amount of co-operation their husbands give in the home is small in comparison with the help the American woman expects as a right. However, in France and Belgium women benefit from a complete network of free nursery schools of a very high standard, run by trained personnel, which accept children from two to six years of age and if necessary will care for them from eight a.m. to six p.m. Although these institutions are numerous and cater for seventy per cent of children between the ages of four and six, they are overwhelmed with applications and have to operate a policy of giving priority to working mothers. On the other hand, kindergartens are fewer in

162

the United States, and even in Great Britain they are often fee-paying and will not take children for more than a few hours each day. Such provisions clearly play a crucial role during the period in which young women finish their studies and take up a career, which is also the time when in general they have young children and modest resources. Thus the Finnish success in recruiting professional women is backed up by a well-organised system of nurseries. In Sweden also great efforts have been made in this direction over the last ten years and it is perhaps to this fact that one might attribute the increased number of women in higher education and professional life. In Germany and Austria, although there are many female workers and a long tradition of female employment, the universities hardly open their doors to women students and are far more restrictive than in other countries. It is as if German society were reluctant to award to her industrious women the professional advancement to which they have a just claim. Apart from this, the school hours in Germany are particularly ill-adapted to the requirements of the working mothers, since the schoolday is over by one p.m. Perhaps this fact in itself explains why so few married women work in Germany compared with other countries and why so many educated women stop work on the birth of their first child and never again take up the professional life.

Italian anti-feminism is traditional but by no means straight-forward, since women control the home much as they do in the United States – for all the obvious differences between the *mamma* and the *momma*. The situation is beginning to change: the labour market is still not very favourable to women, above all those who are poor or untrained, but it is becoming more open to educated young women, who have doubled their proportion of university places over the last fifteen years and have become much more receptive to new ideas. Compared to its neighbour Switzerland, the bastion of anti-feminism, this change seems striking and may be expected to increase.

INDÉPENDANTES.

— Eh bien! moi aussi je vais au club.

Discrimination in appointment

Before leaving this subject we must not pass over the discrimination against women that operates at the stage of advertising vacant posts and of making appointments.

The recent American practice was to announce posts for men and women separately. Such advertisements were presented in two separate columns under the headings: *Help wanted Men, Help wanted Women.* Under the Civil Rights Bill of 1964, the well-known Article 7 condemns any discrimination based on race, religion or sex. But although this practice has become illegal, it is difficult to eradicate. This type of discrimination also operates in Great Britain although less systematically than in America. Thus, a small investigation published in *New Society* (August 1964) examined 626 adverts appearing in two Sunday papers. Of these 198 explicitly stated that only men need apply, while only forty-seven invited both male and female applicants. The remainder were unspecific and the author of the enquiry checked with 178 of these advertisers

A woman in a responsible job must be
able to offer more qualifications
and skills than a man, while at the
same time remaining 'feminine'.

165

as to whether a woman could apply. It appeared that lack of explicitness often concealed discrimination, as prospective employers answered that they were unwilling to consider applications from women. Their replies were interesting in themselves, since they stressed the exclusion of women from higher posts. For instance, 'It is not the policy of our advanced projects group to appoint women to senior technical positions', or 'Although the duties of the advertised post could undoubtedly be carried out by a suitably qualified woman, the activities to which this position will lead compel us to appoint a man.'

An interesting survey has been carried out in France on the women graduating from the Political Science Institute of the University of Paris since 1945. The diploma of this Institute generally leads to higher executive posts and is naturally the same for men and women students. Yet many female informants mentioned that their prospective employers had asked whether they could type, while this was never asked of a man. The average monthly salary of women graduates after several years of work was between 1,500 and 2,000 francs, whereas that for men graduating in the same years averaged about 3,000 francs, and this despite the fact that both sexes had had the same training and received an identical degree.

Professional women and male virility

To discuss this matter one may appeal to innumerable studies and a wealth of detail, the most unexpected of which come from the People's Democracies. Thus Czech women, for instance, assert that they are discriminated against as soon as they leave university to take up their first post. Similarly in the USSR women often complain vigorously of having to make do with second-rate posts while the most interesting appointments are given to men. Yet their position is comparably better than that of western women for entering the professions and achieving success in their careers. In this connection one can but ask whether Soviet men have the worldwide reputation of lacking virility, of being hen-

pecked, of having been castrated and tamed, of being mere drones never able to match their women in inventiveness, creativity and stamina. While there are as many stereotypes of the Soviet man as there are positions on the political spectrum, this particular view has never been put forward simply because it is unsubstantiated by facts. The husbands of these doctors, engineers and economists of renown are not psychologically impaired by their wives' success nor are their sons made to feel inadequate. This state of affairs is not viewed as abnormal, and even the American authority on child-rearing, Dr Spock, confirms that its results are not damaging, since the offspring of these highly successful Russian mothers have fewer problems than the western children with non-working, family centred mothers. On the other hand the long-drawn-out joke of the submissive husband is an integral part of American self-criticism. The dominating wife and the dominated husband,

A 'round table' on the cinema in Montreal, including Agnes Varda (director of *Cleo from 5 to 7*, *Le Bonheur*, etc).

167

who signs the cheques and does the washing up, are legion in comics and films. Yet there is only a very small minority of American women who reach the highest posts and carry great responsibility in professional life. All the same, American men are afraid and communicate their fear to western men in general, whereas the Russians and Finns seem immune from such fear. Only one conclusion can be drawn from this contrast, namely that there is no association between women's occupational advancement and men's loss of status. Perhaps on the contrary a woman who has been deprived of outlets in professional life will channel her frustrated energies into challenging her husband's authority in the home. She may seek to rule her family, and in the process may, to quote an old author, 'strangle her husband and sons with her apron-strings', with that very apron under which she used to shelter her children. Her excess energy may also be directed towards being obsessively house-proud, thus taking a masochistic turn which will make life more difficult for the whole family.

The advancement and the emancipation of women are distinct from each other although related. The progress of women in education, work, creativity, culture, political and social affairs is undoubtedly less shocking for men than their sexual emancipation – which men at once aid and resist. In our societies, professional advancement and sexual emancipation often seem to be moving forward together. This is not always the case. Thus in China, for example, the last fifteen years have brought about remarkable occupational progress for women, although throughout this period Chinese women have remained the most reserved and moralistic members of a society itself hostile to permissiveness and promiscuity.

It has often been suggested that in the field of education women have crossed the immense gap which historically separated them from men. In the past, knowledge was the prerogative of men while women were kept in a state of ignorance; today both sexes are said to have equal access to learning.

In fact there are in the world today about one thousand million illiterates of whom at a conservative estimate over 700 million are women. Perhaps in terms of absolute numbers there have never been so many illiterates nor so many more illiterate women than men. The percentages of female illiteracy in underdeveloped countries in the 'sixties are a staggering illustration of this fact (see table 6:1). Thus in Africa nine women out of ten are illiterate. Differences in relation to percentages of male illiteracy are considerable: there are twenty per cent more literate men than women

Table 6:1 Percentages of female illiteracy in Africa

Algeria	94	Malawi	75
Burundi	93	Mali	99
Cameroon	93	Morocco	94
Central African Republic	99	Niger	99
Congo (Brazzaville)	97	Nigeria	94
Congo (Republic)	87	Rwanda	91
Dahomey	96	Senegal	98
Ethiopia	96	Somaliland	100
Gabon	95·5	Sudan	97
Ghana	90	Tanzania	95
Guinea	96	Tunisia	96
Ivory Coast	98	Uganda	74
Kenya	90	United Arab Republic	88
Liberia	95·8	Upper Volta	99
Libya	95·8	Zambia	70·3
Madagascar	85		

Note: these percentages are now decreasing owing to improved schooling

In 1914 eighty-eight per cent of Soviet women could
not read or write. It has taken only forty years to
eliminate this illiteracy. The picture shows women
in the North Caucasus region in 1929.

in Ghana, Gabon, Kenya, Nigeria, Sudan, Tunisia and Uganda,
and over twenty per cent in Cameroon, Congo (Brazzaville),
Libya, Malawi, Mauritius, United Arab Republic and Zambia.

Outside Africa there are even greater differences between male
and female rates of literacy. Discrepancies as great as those found
in table 6:2 also exist in Bolivia, Ceylon, Korea, Iran, Iraq,
Jordan and Thailand – in the last two countries the rate of female
illiteracy is double that of male. Even in Europe where literacy
is almost universal, the residue of illiterates consists largely of
women. Thus in Greece 30 per cent of women and only 8·3 per
cent of men are illiterate; in Portugal the rate of female illiteracy is
44·6 per cent and in Albania 36·4 per cent, Yugoslavia has 33·6 per
cent women and 12·4 per cent men who are illiterate – Bulgaria
21·9 per cent women and 7·3 per cent men, and Spain 17·7 per cent
women and 8·4 per cent men.

Table 6:2 Difference between male and female illiteracy rates

Country	Percentage of illiterate males	Percentage of illiterate females	Approx. amount more female than male illiterates
Cambodia	22·3	75·4	3½ times
Burma	20	60	3 ,,
Hongkong	9·8	48·2	5 ,,
Peru	25·6	52·4	2 ,,
Turkey	45	78·9	1½ ,,
Formosa	27	56	2 ,,
India	58·5	86·8	½ ,,
Indonesia	42·8	70·4	1½ ,,
Israel	9·5	22	2½ ,,

The vital need to educate women

The great majority of these illiterate women are adults who are condemned to die without having known how to read or write. The only means of reducing the educational gap between the sexes appears to be the introduction of compulsory schooling for all children, girls as well as boys, regardless of previous tradition. However, the tide of illiteracy is running so high that it becomes increasingly difficult to stem by building schools, more schools and yet more schools. But the will to educate exists and the example of Russia is eminently encouraging. Before the First World War eighty-eight per cent of Russian women were illiterate and contemporary educationalists anticipated that it would take 250 years to universalise literacy. In fact in less than fifty years the task has been accomplished.

Today it is recognised that a society which neglects the education of its women does so at its peril. Indeed no policy of birth control can succeed if women remain steeped in ignorance and superstition. Unless the educational level of women is raised, one cannot rely on chemical and other methods of contraception to reduce the population expansion which is so inimical to economic progress in many countries. A woman who has no status in her family, among in-laws, in her tribe or in her village unless she has an appreciable number of male offspring (her girl children will be counted as surplus) will not seek to plan her family. She cannot even desire to limit her family size until she considers herself an individual, a creature totally different from a field which must bear a crop, until passive reproduction is replaced by active child-rearing. The implication of the question 'How many children would you like to have?' eludes these millions of illiterate women who are incapable of seeing their life as a whole and of deciding on their optimum family size. The very notion of time is difficult for them and that of planning even more incomprehensible. Thus the demographic evolution of the world and consequently its economic and social progress depend, to a large extent, on female education.

The war on want and malnutrition which is being fought for

half the world's population again requires women to be educated. It is no good importing foodstuffs rich in protein, such as fishmeal, if mothers, through ignorance or superstition, are too ignorant to give these to their children. In some regions, women refuse to cook vegetables which grow abundantly in their neighbourhood because of the traditional magical beliefs attached to these plants, and only education can change such behaviour patterns.

To educate the masses of illiterate women is not philanthropy undertaken in a spirit of egalitarian idealism or as a democratic crusade. It is a vital need in the modern world, a question of life or death for many, and for all a choice between stagnation and progress. Without female education, progress can be transmitted to each generation either not at all or very slowly, since it cannot be passed on in the home. This may seem exaggerated and over-emphatic, but the case cannot be made too strongly. UNESCO realises the overwhelming importance of basic education for women as well as for men. Without this, the world of tomorrow, despite its scientists and its astronauts, will be overpopulated and will suffer more poverty, malnutrition and illiteracy than ever before.

The tidal wave of female ignorance must be stopped in this generation. Great progress seems to have been made, despite the the fact that most efforts result merely in preventing a deterioration of the existing situation. In the middle of the twentieth century the United Nations proclaimed compulsory schooling for children of both sexes. Twenty years later there remain 43·4 per cent of children of school age who receive no education, and the great majority of them are girls.

Attendance at primary schools

In 1961, UNESCO launched a large-scale investigation on primary school attendance. Out of the eighty-five countries covered, fifty-one counted over forty-six per cent of girls among school attenders – a reasonably good record. However, in twenty-four countries girls represented only ten to forty per cent of primary school pupils. Furthermore, this situation is probably much worse in the

It is difficult to see how the problem of over-population can
be solved while women in so many countries remain uneducated.
Below This young Egyptian woman has been married for six years.
Right A poster on birth control: 'Frequent pregnancies
produce a weak generation and take toll of the mother and
the family budget' (centre lettering).

وحدات تنظيم الأسرة

في خدمة المواطنين

فهي تعمل على

مكافحة الإجهاض بمنع الحمل الغير مرغوب فيه — **كما تشجع النسل** بعلاج العقم لدى الزوجين

الحمل السريع المتكرر
ينتج جيلاً ضعيفاً هزيلاً
كما يرهق صحة الأم
وميزانية الأسرة

بعكس

الحمل المنظم المتباعد
الفترات ينتج جيلاً قوياً
سليماً ويبقى على صحة
الأم وميزانية الأسرة

نظموا أسرتكم تنعموا بحياة عائلية سعيدة

فالعبرة بالنوع .. وليست بالعدد

وزارة الصحة العمومية - مصلحة الصحة الاجتماعية - قسم الثقافة الصحية والخدمات الاجتماعية

countries that did not answer the investigation. In 1965, of 122 member countries or associate members of UNESCO, only fifty-eight – not even half – had as many girls as boys in primary schools. When, as in many countries, schooling is only compulsory 'in so far as it is possible', it is the boys who go while the girls stay at home and make themselves useful.

Moreover, educational equality, even at the elementary level, is rarely extended to girls except in co-educational schools. Otherwise teaching given solely to girls is often of a lower quality, teachers tend to be less qualified and curricula abbreviated. It is often purely a preparation for the future roles of wife and mother and a debased version of the education given to boys. It is much more frequent for girls than for boys to leave elementary school, presumably under parental pressure, without finishing the full course. Over half of the UNESCO member countries reported this – the range of variation in the withdrawal of girls from primary school being from five to ninety per cent. The reasons most commonly given for early leaving among girls are the requirements of housework and help on the farm.

Despite this, the overall number of female pupils at elementary schools is growing throughout the world. Unfortunately, this growth is more striking in terms of absolute numbers than as a percentage of the total intake. In spite of all the attempts made between 1950 and 1963 to reduce the gap between girls' and boys' primary school attendance, it has only narrowed by one per cent.

Secondary education

Girls are even more under-represented in secondary education because many families see no value in female instruction once the basic three 'r's have been acquired. Some progress has been made, the proportion of girls in secondary schools being considered satisfactory in over half of the member states, mediocre in thirty-eight per cent and distinctly bad in eight per cent. Between 1950 and 1960 the trend has certainly been favourable as forty-eight countries instead of thirty-one now have over forty-six per cent of female

pupils at secondary level. Thus in these countries at least the development of education for girls has been more rapid than for boys over the period, since the gap has been closed. Nevertheless, the situation varies enormously from country to country. For example, in Asia four countries register over forty-six per cent of girls among their secondary school pupils and three less than twenty per cent.

Table 6:4 presents the situation in 1964 for Europe and North America. It should be noted that in eastern Europe as well as the United States the fact that many boys enter vocational training before finishing secondary school accounts for the predominance of girls among secondary pupils. This is also the case in Denmark, Finland, France, Ireland, Sweden and Yugoslavia. In almost all the countries listed, girls have truly achieved parity with boys, since, according to data available for 1965, they account for nearly fifty per cent of those getting secondary school certificates, except in Luxemburg (31·4 per cent), Federal Germany (34·7 per cent), Spain (34·2 per cent) and Belgium (35·9 per cent).

Vocational training

The position of girls in technical and vocational training is considerably less satisfactory than in other branches of education. Even in some developed countries most girls do not remain in secondary education beyond the compulsory leaving age. Those who leave school and begin to work ought to have the same training facilities as boys, which would enable them to qualify, often in a short period of time, before seeking gainful employment.

The idea of occupational training for girls is surrounded by a network of badly reasoned arguments. These facile stereotypes are of no relevance to modern society, but relate only to irrational prejudices on the part of all concerned – families, adolescents themselves, governments and employers. In the long run no one stands to gain from this state of affairs, except a few cold-blooded employers benefiting from a reserve army of personnel whose lack of qualifications makes it possible to pay them very badly to do the most boring jobs.

In many countries, girls are taught to sew and even to embroider on the pretext that 'it will certainly be useful when they marry'. According to a Belgian industrialist, 'qualified embroiderers make excellent assembly workers in the electrical industry, being dexterous and accurate'. Therefore he employed in his factory skilled young women who could not find work in their trade. They were appreciated on another score, namely that, although they were quicker workers than men, they could receive the wage rates of unskilled labour, as their qualifications in embroidery clearly did not count under the collective agreements for the electrical industry. One could mention many such examples. In the French metallurgical industry a good third of women workers are qualified seam-

Table 6:3 Girls as a percentage of the total number of pupils in primary schools and secondary schools

Area	Year	Primary schools	Secondary schools
Africa	1960	36·6	32·3
	1963	37·4	32·9
Asia	1960	38·5	33·1
	1963	38·4	35·2
Europe	1960	48·5	47·8
	1963	48·6	48·3
North America	1960	48·2	49·6
	1963	48·4	49·4
South America	1960	48·2	43·4
	1963	48·6	49·4
Oceania	1960	49·4	47·4
	1963	47·6	47·2
USSR	1958	49·0	55·0

Table 6:4 Girls as a percentage of the total number of secondary school pupils in 1964

Austria	39	Norway	49
Belgium	46	Portugal	48
Denmark	52	Scotland	48
Eire	53	Spain	41
Federal Germany	44	Sweden	54
Finland	54	England and Wales	49
France	52	Yugoslavia	53
Italy	42		
Luxemburg	43	Canada	49
Netherlands	48	Mexico	37

United States exact percentage unavailable but over fifty per cent. Eastern Europe over fifty per cent (Poland sixty-five per cent)

stresses, but paid and classified as unskilled workers. Where changes have been made in the education of women, the replacement of sewing by domestic science is no improvement. Indeed who could say that a girl who has qualified in domestic science is ready to face the labour market?

Parental influence

Parents often prefer to keep their daughters in secondary schools rather than let them train for an occupation. Even if this additional schooling does not lead to higher education, it can be justified by the rather vague reflection that it can't do any harm and that it provides a cultural background before marriage. Sometimes parents hide behind the guarantee that after having attended the *lycée*, *gymnasium*, grammar or high school, their daughters will certainly find some type of office employment. They would never be content with this prospect for their sons. If a youth employment officer asks them directly what employment they and their daughter look to for her future, the great majority display a combination of embarrassment and vagueness. 'Oh you know with a girl . . .' is the traditional opening for the father (if he has bothered to attend the interview at all). Thus parental aspirations tend to be concentrated on sons and less ambition is invested in the daughter's future. But lack of ambition is not synonymous with openness to suggestions. If the employment officer proposes attendance at a technical college or some type of apprenticeship where the girl could learn industrial design or a craft, the parents tend to be amazed and reluctant. The father is incredulous and the mother is horrified at such an unfeminine idea. The outcome depends entirely on the persuasiveness of the officer. To encourage parents to add another unemployed hairdresser to the market would be easy; they prefer to imagine their daughters putting curls into place than assembling electrical circuits. It is considered feminine to dye hair, but not to manufacture hair dyes.

The teenager
The adolescents tend to be their own worst enemies. They do not devote to the choice of an occupation which may be theirs for the rest of their life the amount of thought they willingly give to choosing a new dress. They quickly fall victim to chance pieces of information picked up from a magazine or heard on television – instantly they decide to become beauticians or dieticians, according to the image projected. It is of course unnecessary to say that the mass media do not help girls to make a realistic choice, since they idealise a few fashionable occupations. Even the primary school does nothing in this respect. A content analysis of Swedish school readers shows that while boys will come across sixty occupations described in their compulsory textbooks, girls had only about ten to choose from. Unless a girl has some notion or image, albeit unrealistic and idealised, of the job she wants to do, she will tend to drift and accept any type of employment, all her future expectations being centred upon marriage. Emotionally marriage is her only goal and wherever she turns this will be reinforced, there will be few counter pressures encouraging her to think of other aims. She may even fear that if she chooses a job with a future, it will reduce her chance of marriage. Girls will never pick jobs by asking themselves whether they would like to continue working at this if they did not marry, since the very eventuality is unthinkable. They are so eager to get the ring on their finger and thus become socially acceptable that they will not tempt fate by even considering that they might fail to find a husband. This attitude is culturally induced and is illustrated in another way by the reluctance of engaged girls to specify their preferences or even to choose between different possibilities in life insurance schemes and bank accounts. They do not want to consider what would happen if they were to be divorced or separated from their husbands, they refuse to listen, they refuse to choose, saying that both would show a lack of trust in their married lives.

In many countries, including England, marriage used to debar women from some professions. Even if the legal obstacle has been

eliminated, as is usually the case, it has left behind a residue of attitudes which continue to condition women's expectations. Marriage is a psychological rather than a legal obstacle, young girls tending to see it as the beginning of a new life or of life itself. In this view, everything preceding the ceremony does not really count. It does not seem worthwhile to make plans, since the premarital state is merely a period of waiting for an almost magical change. This common approach has nothing to do with women's nature, it is culturally induced. It does not even arise from being in love, since in our culture girls think of marriage in general long before they fall in love with an individual. Many teenagers look forward only to marriage and this attitude is found among university students as well as among young workers.

Government and employers

Even supposing that the government proclaimed full equality for women, this would not be enough to uproot such deeply embedded attitudes. To most governments, however, such attitudes are not undesirable, since they ensure a body of unskilled workers, pre-

pared to do anything, generally undemanding and weak in collective bargaining. This is never stated in theory, but accepted in practice,
and is explicit in manpower planning. It is difficult to plan the
development of male posts with any exactitude and therefore
advantageous to count on a female work force as a stopgap in
order to fill any non-remunerative jobs unwanted by men and only
fit for unskilled women. As technological change becomes faster,
prospects of female employment are transformed. There is a glut
of simple copy typists and a corresponding lack of bilingual
secretaries and trained documentalists. It is only then that attitudes
to womanpower change and the government realises that it has
at its disposal an untapped pool of girls who can be trained to
staff skilled posts in offices and factories.

However, the employers have a different opinion on this subject.
In many countries, they have to cover a percentage of the cost of
training. As a rule, they are not prepared to make the same contributions for girls as for boys. To them there is little reason in
paying for training or day-release schools when female workers are
likely to leave the job shortly afterwards and have a high record of
absenteeism. It is true that women stay away from work more
than men, if one takes into account short periods of absence and
the poor record of some individuals who influence the average.
However, the studies of Mayo and Lombard in the United States
and of Isambert and Guilbert in France have shown that female
absenteeism was closely associated with lack of qualifications,
which in turn was found to be related to lack of responsibilities at
work, absence of promotion prospects and low wages. A skilled
female worker with responsibilities attached to her post does not
stay away any more than a man in a similar position. Unskilled
women absent themselves as frequently as unskilled immigrant
male workers who too are concentrated in the lowest paid and
least desirable jobs. According to the Hawthorne investigation, a
girl who stayed away from work on eighty-five occasions within
a period of thirty-two months before the experiment started did
not absent herself once in the sixteen months following the intro-

duction of new work methods allowing her more scope for advancement and initiative.

This conjunction of influences gives rise to a vicious circle which is difficult to break, hence the deplorable state of occupational training for women nearly everywhere. The situation seems immutable in some countries, supported as it is by age-old prejudice. Yet in fact to train a young girl properly for a particular job in this technological age is the best way to preserve her femininity. It is certainly better than to send her straight from school into a factory where she will have to do the most monotonous and stultifying jobs or into a bar or canteen where she will have to put up with uncivil customers and where she will be tempted to seek a way out at any cost.

It is mainly in Sweden and Federal Germany that efforts have been made to improve training prospects for young girls. In France too since 1966 almost all the vocational schools previously reserved to boys have become co-educational. Certainly before that date the French provisions were wholly inadequate and it is still too soon to judge the effectiveness of the 1966 reform. In Britain, the Industrial Training Act has brought about measures of change, but there are still grave disparities between the possibilities for boys and for girls. There are considerable sex differentials in attendance at training courses, particularly after eighteen years of age, and this seems to reflect social attitudes rather than parliamentary legislation.

The traditional image of women's role is the main obstacle which prevents her adapting to the modern world. This image prevails at all levels and leads to the universal statement: 'Women are incapable of. . .'. Yet, after a time, they are found doing the work for which it was alleged that they could not be trained. But they get the job only after it has ceased to confer any prestige on its holder. A historical perspective shows that there is no better index of the discrepancy between male and female employment prospects than access to vocational training.

Higher education

The status of women in higher education is quite different from their position in vocational training. For a start it is the girls with the greatest ability and often also with the strongest motivation who are recruited by the universities. Such girls tend to place a high premium on their own intellectual development. On the other hand, there are great international differences in the proportion of women undertaking higher education. While vocational instruction for girls tends to be universally discouraged, except perhaps in the USSR, there are considerable disparities from country to country in the composition of the student body. Thus the UNESCO Conference held at Vienna in November 1967 to consider cross-national comparisons of the problems faced by Ministers of Education in member countries found three specific features of higher education.

1 Some countries have a very democratic policy of easy access to higher education, while others operate a rigid system of selection to recruit an élite. Because of this, the ratio of students of both sexes to the total population is highly variable.

2 Therefore one should always consider girl students as a percentage of the total population rather than in absolute numbers. Otherwise one cannot tell whether a small number of girl students merely reflects a general restrictive policy at the level of university entry or whether it results from discrimination against women.

3 Even if one finds that both in absolute and relative terms the intake of girls is high, this offers no guarantee of female parity within higher education, unless they are evenly distributed over the full range of disciplines. It is significant to see which faculties receive most female students and in which degree-courses they are most numerous. It is only in this way then , that some idea can be gained of the progress of women towards élite positions and of the break with traditional cultural patterns which is likely to occur in the next few decades.

Tables 6:5 and 6:6 show the discrepancies which exist in this respect in Europe. The ratio of female students to the total popula-

A nineteenth-century German satire:
the 'modern' housewife. Reprinted
from *The Graphic*, 1882.

THE RENAISSANCE OF THE RENAISSANCE — THE MODERN HOUSEWIFE

Table 6:5 Number of female students in higher education

Country	Female students per 100,000 inhabitants	Total number of female students
USSR	1,427	1,660,015
Finland	862	20,627
Czechoslovakia	767	54,764
France	696 (Univ. only)	173,360
Sweden	630 ,, ,,	24,500
Yugoslavia	619	62,011
Belgium	583	28,004
Poland	582	94,400
Netherlands	539	33,394
Romania	528	51,360
Eire	452	6,487
United Kingdom	427	119,649
Hungary	412	21,611
Italy	395	105,736
Denmark	377	10,300
Greece	358	not provided
Austria	260	10,029
Federal Germany	258	84,200
Norway	253	4,725
Switzerland	196	5,751
Spain	181	29,690
Turkey	124	18,909

NB The figure provided for the USSR includes women studying for degrees both by correspondence course and as evening students. The statistics for Sweden and France are only for university students, to the exclusion of other establishments for higher education after eighteen, e.g. teacher training in France is given in special colleges outside the university (*écoles normales*).

The State University in Rio de Janeiro. In the vast majority of countries girls are now free to enter university but the majority choose arts subjects. Science is still a masculine preserve in most western countries (see tables 6:8 and 6:9).

tion or to the population between twenty and twenty-four years may even be ten times greater in one country than in another. These international differences are more pronounced than for male students. Thus it is impossible to speak of chances of entry into higher education for European girls, since these vary not only according to individual ability, effort, and social origin, but also with country or residence. As we have seen, the number of working women in any given country depends more on the level of economic development than on the prevailing view of woman's role. However, this does not hold for the numbers of women entering higher education – economic pressures in favour of its extension being much weaker than parental prejudice against it, particularly in the countries where public opinion is opposed to educated women. These views can be summed up as follows: 'Studying cannot make a woman happy', 'Women are out of place

Table 6:6 Number of female students in higher education per 100 people aged between twenty and twenty-four years in 1965

Bulgaria	15·2	Hungary	5·8
France	12·4	Italy	5·6
Finland	11·3	Denmark	5·3
Poland	10·0	Greece	5·3
Belgium	9·9	Federal Germany	4·3
Sweden	8·2	Austria	3·9
Romania	7·8	Norway	3·9
Yugoslavia	7·6	Switzerland	2·3
Netherlands	7·0	Spain	1·9 (1960)
Eire	6·6	Turkey	1·5
United Kingdom	6·6		

Table 6:7 Percentage of girls among students

Finland	49	Yugoslavia	34
Bulgaria	43	Belgium	33
USSR	43	Denmark	31
France	42	Canada	28 †
Hungary	42	Spain	27
USA	39 *	Austria	25
Romania	39	Netherlands	25
Czechoslovakia	39	Federal Germany	24
United Kingdom	38	Norway	24
Poland	38	Turkey	21
Italy	36	Switzerland	19
Sweden	35		

* data of the Office of Education for 1965.
† assessment for part of 1968 intake.

Women are now admitted into science, but they usually occupy the lower ranks, such as that of laboratory assistant, as here.

Figure 9 Bachelor's degrees earned by women.

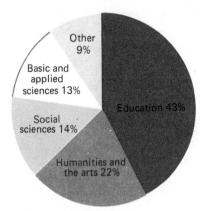

in positions of authority', 'Men do not fall for bluestockings'. Similar statements can be found in the investigation on the status of women carried out in 1966 by the German Bundestag: 'The university is meant for men', 'Intelligence is a male prerogative', 'Neither logical thinking nor an education designed for men is suited to women'.

It is impossible to assess the impact of attitudinal factors on women's entry into higher education. However, perhaps one can assume that the closer one gets to fifty per cent of students being female, the more likely it is that attitudes to women's access are favourable and chances of entry are the same for both sexes.

The resistance to girls' entry into higher education is obvious in some countries, such as the Netherlands, despite the fact that the university system is open and the percentage of students in the population high. Similarly in the Federal Republic, Austria, Norway, Switzerland and Turkey, girls represent under a quarter of university students. It is in the People's Democracies, Finland and France that they account for more than forty per cent of

Table 6:8 Percentage of women students in each faculty

	Year	Letters	Teaching	Fine Art	Law
Austria	1964	49·3	35·0	47·3	16·0
Belgium	1964	41·7	62·0	21·3	16·5
Czechoslavakia	1965	66·9	48·9	37·9	54·9
Denmark	1964	51·9	54·6	30·3	29·4
Eire	1965	36·1	70·5	31·9	18·0
Federal Germany	1965	39·3	62·2	42·4	11·2
Finland	1965	75·5	55·0	30·5	26·8
France	1965	64·9			28·2
Hungary	1965	68·7	79·6	43·6	52·4
Italy	1965	65·9	77·7	26·0	16·4
Netherlands	1964	39·1	51·0		23·5
Norway	1963	40·1	29·4	22·1	7·7
Poland	1965	67·0	56·5	44·9	37·7
Romania	1964	60·3	55·0	43·3	18·3
Spain	1963	61·6	65·2	16·7	12·0
Sweden	1961	50·7	50·3		17·3
Switzerland	1965	41·3	51·7	13·2	11·7
Turkey	1965	39·2	24·8	33·1	25·0
United Kingdom					
England and Wales	1964	64·5			
Scotland	1961		83·0		
Northern Ireland	1964	44·2	64·9	40·9	13·8
USSR	1964/65		64		
Yugoslavia	1965	56·9	45·3	40·5	29·6

Note: blank spaces indicate incomplete data.

Social sciences	Sciences	Engi- neering	Medicine	Agri- culture	Total
19·3	25·4	4·7	31·6	8·2	23·9
30·6	24·8	0·6	41·1	3·2	32·4
53·2	65·4	14·3	62·5	26·0	38·2
18·5	22·5	4·4	31·5	7·3	36·1
22·7	27·4	11·1	24·1	2·3	30·5
12·5	13·3	1·8	29·8	12·5	23·6
43·3	37·4	3·6	48·8	39·0	49·1
	30·4		34·5		41·3
53·4	58·8	18·7	51·3	19·0	42·4
27·9	31·9	0·5	18·3	2·9	35·5
12·6	12·2	1·3	19·4	12·9	17·9
7·1	17·3	2·5	19·6	6·5	22·4
38·5	57·6	14·7	63·5	32·8	37·5
33·8	51·7	21·0	54·7	20·6	38·4
15·6	24·7	0·8	20·6	2·0	20·7
25·9	26·6	4·4	32·6	9·2	34·3
11·5	15·1	0·8	21·4	5·5	19·8
18·4	23·2	7·2	23·4	13·0	21·2
23·0	21·7	1·2	26·0	13·1	38·0
	37·8				56·4
31·3	16·3	1·9	25·4	5·9	33·5
	29·0	52·0			
34·3	39·6	13·9	50·1	14·7	33·5

The modern phenomenon of the young student/mother has meant that the man has learned to share the traditional maternal tasks.

Table 6:9 Percentage of master's degrees gained by women in the USA in 1964

Subject	Percentage	Total number
Education	46·3	18,841
Arts and letters	36·3	5,727
Social sciences	22·4	2,181
Sciences	10·0	3,228

student intake. Once again Scandinavia varies from country to country – Finland's completely egalitarian policy provides a total contrast with Norway whose universities remain largely closed to women, while Sweden and Denmark are situated somewhere between these extremes, despite their overall low intake of women. In conclusion one should note that in several countries the proportion of women students has risen steadily since 1965.

Some student characteristics
The social origins of women students tend to be quite different from those of men, being biased towards the upper social strata.

The higher income groups can afford to let their daughters take advantage of the cultural life at university without much concern for future careers. By contrast there are even fewer girls than boys from the lower socio-economic groups, where traditional attitudes are more enduring and financial resources often insufficient to finance the education of more than one child, preferably male. Even in France, where women's· entry to higher education is encouraged, social distinctions operate against them more than

against men, particularly at the lowest socio-economic levels.

Moreover, the subjects studied at degree level also provide a distinction between male and female students. Girls tend to opt for those courses leading to a career in teaching, such as education, languages and arts. In the faculties of letters they outnumber men. A significant proportion of women choose medical studies, particularly in the People's Democracies where they predominate. The applied sciences (engineering) are still a masculine domain in western Europe but attract many female students in the Soviet Union. Unlike most other countries, Finland has many women studying agronomy (see table 6:8).

It is difficult to draw a comparison between European and American data. The number of female students is remarkably high in the United States, but the definition of 'student' is not the same. Thus all girls in teacher training colleges are counted as students, which is not the case in France. Similarly courses leading to a diploma in home economics are not part of higher education in Europe and First Professional Degrees are considered as a form of vocational training. The concentration of girls in education, arts

The Second Solvay Conference at Brussels, 1913,
with Madame Curie the only woman among such male
eminences as Einstein, Lorentz and Rutherford.
Before her, the woman scientist did not exist.

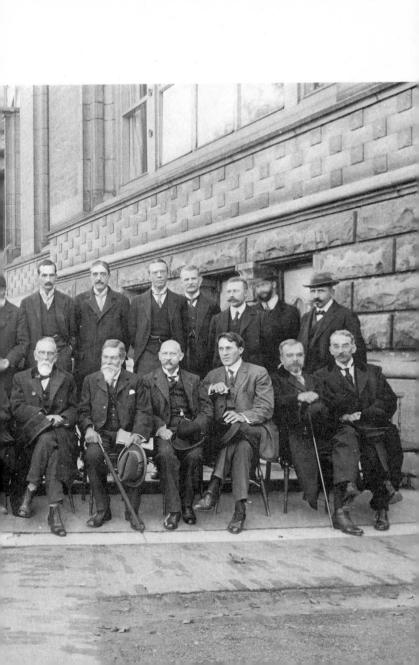

and social sciences is even greater in the States than in Europe, as is their absence from science faculties. Figure 9 (page 191) gives the breakdown of subjects studied by women at the BA level.

The picture changes in postgraduate studies, as table 6:9 shows. The Canadian situation is largely the same. Thus there is a reduction in the concentration of girls in studies of home economics and correspondingly a slight increase in the female intake of science faculties. However, on the whole American girls undertake higher education to fit them better for some very feminine occupation or to become more cultivated. This is borne out by the fact that very few women indeed continue their studies to doctorate level, which is almost essential in America for a professional career. The proportion of women doctoral students is not increasing and in fact has dropped since 1930, when they obtained 15·4 per cent of doctorates awarded in all subjects, whereas they only secured 10·5 per cent in 1960 and 10·6 per cent in 1964.

A similar weeding out of female students throughout the successive stages of higher education is also found in Federal Germany, the Netherlands and Denmark. However, in other countries women do not differ from men in this respect. Marriage is the main cause of discontinued studies. In the last years there has been a paradoxical conjunction of increase in the numbers of female students and decrease in the age of marriage for girls. Once again it seems clear that the main obstacles to women's careers are not directly related to their work, but to their family life. It is not so much that women lose interest in their studies when they marry, but rather that they find it difficult to be students and housewives at the same time. Increasingly those countries most favourably disposed towards working women provide facilities for married students to help them over this difficult period. Nevertheless, it is much more difficult for a girl to complete a very long course of study than it is for a man. Everything conspires to encourage the efforts of male students and to discourage women whose perseverance is construed as useless or even selfish.

Professional employment of graduates

It is generally true that women graduates have higher rates of employment than those who have only received primary schooling. In all countries the percentage of women graduates who work, even while they have small children, is remarkably high: seventy-two per cent in the United States, eighty per cent in France, and at comparable levels elsewhere. Therefore it would not be true to suppose that the investment in higher education for women, the cost of which is often borne by the state, is wasted. On the contrary, the best educated women tend to go on working, while the least educated are less likely to do so (on average only twenty-five per cent of them remain in employment). However, in some countries which do not welcome women on the labour market or in higher education, at least half if not more of the women who gain degrees do not work. This is true of Switzerland, the Netherlands and Spain. Curiously then it is the countries which admit most women to their universities which are best repaid by the susequent occupational activities of these graduates. Conversely, it is those countries which admit few women into higher education whose investment is least repaid.

7 The law

It would be a mistake to assume that the fight for female emancipation only began at the end of the eighteenth century with the efforts of Mary Wollstonecraft and Olympe de Gouges, before reaching its climax in the late nineteenth and early twentieth centuries with the suffragettes. Much earlier in history women sought step by step to gain for themselves those rights which men had won with the progress of democracy. When serfdom was abolished and citizenship established during the French Revolution, women demanded the same civil rights as men. They could have had no such claims throughout the feudal age and under the absolute monarchy, since many men were deprived of civic rights while some women of aristocratic birth possessed power, acted as judges, held fiefs, received taxes and generally ruled the lives of their subjects. It was only when the principle and later the practice of universal male suffrage became current, when parliamentary democracy became established, that women demanded enfranchisement. The militant suffragettes did not emerge all at once from a state of bondage, nor were men suddenly overcome by a sense of remorse which led them to concede these new demands. Throughout history there has been a constant interplay between a vanguard of women, aware of the growing lag between the condition of the two sexes in society, and the rearguard of men who wish, in practice if not in theory, to prevent male rights being applied also to women. This process still applies to modern society. In times of rapid change it is men who win new rights for themselves, but it is women who seek to make them universal rather than only male. Women's claims are justified by their share in collective effort and hardship. In wartime it is women who step in and take over basic services, while men are at the front. In resistance movements and struggles against occupying or colonial powers, women invariably play a large part. Consequently, after the Second World War and the accession to independence of many former colonies, the rights of man increased throughout the world and women had a share in this process. As far as women are concerned, the post-war period witnessed very rapid progress. Each month the newly created United Nations Organisation accorded new rights to women. This period of emancipation was followed by a phase of consolidation in most countries and of slight deterioration in some. Thus today one can try to draw up a balance sheet of the rights obtained by women, the inequalities which persist between the sexes, and the extent to which women make use of their new-found freedoms.

The right to vote
Women's suffrage has been their greatest achievement in the twentieth century. In 1900 only one country (Australia) allowed women the vote in all elections. In 1918 this example was followed by twelve other countries and in 1945 women had the vote in forty states; at present there are 106 states in which both sexes have the right to vote and to stand as representatives. Almost all the newly independent states established in former colonies accepted this principle and thus achieved overnight a situation which had taken the economically and politically more developed countries much longer to attain.

The history of female suffrage includes some strange paradoxes. Governments committed to a left-wing ideology have been theoretically in favour of female emancipation, but have feared that women's votes would benefit their conservative or reactionary opponents. They tended to think that the mass of women without political experience, fearful and priest-ridden, constantly seeking security, would be bound to vote against the left. Instead of attempting to win female votes by a policy of rapid education and by adopting platforms which would make them popular with women, some of these governments have preferred to declare women eligible for election yet without allowing them the right to vote. This was the case of the socialist government in Belgium, while the French *Front Populaire* named female ministers without granting women the vote. Their political opponents, less favourable in theory to women's emancipation, drew the moral from these socialist qualms, so that often a conservative government

Women suffragettes *c.* 1910. They created a scandal by demanding a right which has since, in many countries, become a duty.

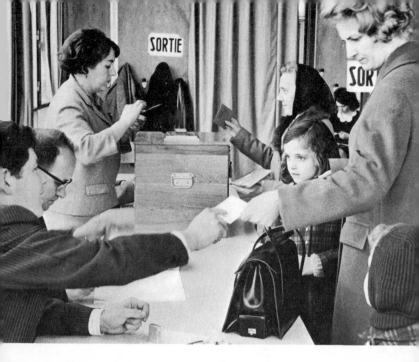

hoping for their electoral support gave women the franchise.

Today the only countries in which women are excluded from voting are: Afghanistan, Iraq, Jordan, Kuwait, Liechtenstein Northern Nigeria, Saudi Arabia, Switzerland and the Yemen. (In Saudi Arabia and the Yemen male suffrage does not exist either.) Switzerland is thus the only western country to continue a policy of male suffrage and in this finds itself in the company of traditional Moslem states. The French-speaking cantons of Geneva, Vaud and Neuchâtel, Valais and the Italian-speaking Tessin have allowed women to vote and stand for elections at the municipal and canton level. Periodically at federal level a referendum is held on the subject of universal suffrage, but each time the men turn it down (mainly in the German-speaking part of the country). Public opinion polls enable one to access the attitudes of women themselves. In German-speaking Switzerland it is only by a small majority that they favour universal suffrage, whereas in the French-speaking regions they clamour for the vote.

In several states women's right to vote is subject to regulations

Women voting in Paris.
The right of being a citizen
is now taken for granted.

205

which are not applied to men. In Guatemala, Portugal and Syria, they are subject to restrictions on educational grounds. In the Sudan women can be elected, but cannot vote, whereas in San Marino the reverse is true. In Brazil voting is obligatory for all men, but only for those women who are gainfully employed. In Ecuador it is compulsory for men, but optional for women. Pakistan is alone in reserving some parliamentary seats to women in both the national and the provincial assemblies.

The United Nations

Through the Commission on the Status of Women constituted in 1946 to further equal rights for women, UNO has greatly contributed to the rapid change which has taken place in this respect. The UN has always stood for a democratic and egalitarian ideology which, while abstract in formulation, has always served as a point of reference for the member states. It has always defended the interests of women, regardless of regional customs and national economic policies. Gradually, despite the artificiality of international meetings in luxurious surroundings, despite underlying hostility, struggles behind the scenes and verbal battles, despite the heavy boredom which seems to emanate from their work and their publications, international organisations – for all the time they seem to waste – have slowly elaborated an international philosophy of respect for the weak, concern for the future of all, tolerance and awareness that all human problems are interdependent.

UNO has made several attempts to define an international declaration on the status of women. First of all, in 1948 the Declaration of the Universal Rights of Man condemned all discrimination based on sex. However, it may be deplored that it did not denounce prostitution and the sale of women with the same vehemence with which it attacked slavery. It is also a source of regret that the right of couples to decide whether to have children and how many, did not figure in the declaration, despite the fact that both the UN and UNESCO are favourably disposed towards it.

The Commission on the Status of Women puts forward recommendations to member states, but has met with great difficulties in implementing its aims. It succeeded in having the proposals of the convention on the Political Rights of Women adopted in 1952 and, from 1959 onwards, member states have every two years submitted a report on progress made in this direction, using as indices the number of women nominated or appointed for certain posts and break-downs of female representation in political bodies.

Lastly the Commission has sought to draw to the notice of international opinion the fact that certain signatories of the Charter affirming equal rights for men and women continue to practise discrimination against women. Accordingly a resolution was adopted in 1967 by the General Assembly on the Elimination of Discriminatory Practices against Women, which demanded that sexual equality of rights be incorporated into national constitutions or guaranteed in law. It also requested that legal provisions should ensure the same rights for both sexes in voting, access to public employment, retention of nationality, acquisition and management of property, freedom of movement, the ability to enter into legal transactions, to marry and to divorce freely, and to exercise the same control over children as is enjoyed by the children's father. If these provisions have been vigorously advocated, this in itself indicates they do not exist in reality, as is clearly shown by the reports drawn up by the Commission on the Status of Women.

Legal discrimination

In private law there is a curious dichotomy which can be traced back to Rousseau, if not to the Romans: there are two legal statuses for women (and this is not only true of countries whose law is derived from Roman law). One status applies to the spinster, the other to the married woman. The spinster, despite her sex, often enjoys all the rights of a man, since she can enter into legal transactions, dispose of property, have a name and a nationality of her own, and the freedom to come and go as she pleases. In this, her 'weakness', 'impressionability' and 'incapacity to reason' seem to have been forgotten, except in the East where the spinster does not possess the same rights as men. However, in the vast majority of western European states and in the People's Democracies the spinster is treated like a man, except in Spain where women do not fully come of age until twenty-five, while men attain their majority at twenty-one. Therefore it is generally assumed that women have sufficient understanding and intelligence to have as much individual independence as men.

However, when the spinster, this reasonable creature, marries, she instantly becomes a minor of sub-average intelligence in the eyes of the law. Or is one to assume that only mentally deficient females ever marry? The man who marries retains his rights, his name and his nationality; whereas in many countries the wife does not have the right to choose her nationality, this being determined for her by that of her husband. She may not even have the right to choose her place of residence, but only to follow her husband. The Roman wife's commitment to cling to her husband, expressed by the saw *Ubi Gaius, ibi Gaia*, did not imply any reciprocity. It may be interpreted as an expression of love, but the law is not designed for lovers. In any case, it would have been more accurate, if less poetic, to use the formula *Ubi ego Gaius, eris tu Gaia*. The married woman gives her husband children, but in many countries the father can dispose of them without her authorisation, and his permission to register them in a school or take them abroad is all that is required – despite the mother's natural capacity for bringing up her young and pursuing their best interests. In several countries the wife cannot dispose of her own property and in some it automatically becomes part of her husband's estate. If the wife is unfaithful to her husband, the consequences are often more serious than those attending male infidelity. Under many legal codes, more stringent penalties are meted out to female adultery than those reserved to men. Thus in Tunisia, which under President Bourguiba pursued a policy of female emancipation, the announcement of equal punishment for adultery for both sexes gave rise to public criticism, because of the extraordinary severity of the punishments. Without needing to search for examples in Africa and the East, there are countries where the jealous husband can kill his wife without severe reprisals, since this is considered to be a crime of honour.

Not only do women lose many rights by marrying, they are not always free to decide whether they wish to wed – and to whom they wish to sacrifice their independence. There are still many countries where arranged marriages prevail.

Discrimination and the married woman

While this picture may appear sombre, it must not be forgotten that few countries enforce all types of discrimination against the married woman. At the same time, however, there is no country which deprives the married man of the rights that he had enjoyed as a bachelor.

The Scandinavian countries are particularly liberal in their treatment of the married woman, whereas those states which adopted the Napoleonic code tend to be the most restrictive. The latter may have amended the law on marriage settlements or on divorce, as is the case in France, but there are still some forms of inequality left. Discrimination is most pronounced in Moslem law countries. To gain an idea of the strength of resistance to female legal equality, one need only cite the fact that out of the 120 UN member states, only twenty-nine have adopted the Convention's recommendation that a woman marrying a foreigner should be free to choose her nationality. Even the Common Market countries have not been able to reach agreement on this issue. A woman may either retain or lose her nationality upon marriage and this may vary with the nationality of the man she marries. Within western Europe there are differences from country to country in the extent to which a married woman can manage her own property and in her authority over her children.

On an international level, the Convention on women's consent to their marriage, minimum age of girls at marriage and legal obligation to register all marriages, was only signed by nineteen member states.

It is often alleged by lawyers that those legal provisions which discriminate against women have fallen into disuse, since they are no longer enforced. Thus, for example, the adultery clauses in the Napoleonic code which imposed a fine on men only if adultery was committed in the conjugal home, while women were punished by imprisonment in all circumstances. But then, why are they retained? The general philosophy which emerges from these different legal texts is that of the Romans, albeit diluted. The female sex is seen on the one hand as submissive, dependent, in need of a master, on the other as treacherous, always ready to rebel and in need of taming. So weak-kneed that it must always be guided or so headstrong that it must be disciplined, the female character eludes legal definition.

However, the 'spirit of the law' has undergone an evolution. Marriage settlements have been reformed completely or partially in France, Belgium, Italy and even Spain. The Spanish law of 1958 amending the Civil Code affirmed that 'the law will not countenance any form of discrimination based on sex'. Yet the 1961 law on political and occupational rights for women retained a legal obligation for the married woman seeking to work either as an employee or as self-employed to provide herself with written permission from her husband. Nor can Spanish married women freely enter into legal transactions, although, curiously enough, Spain is the only country in Europe where women retain their maiden name after marriage.

All these provisions are backed up by an *a priori* assumption of woman's subjection to man, a postulate whose irrationality was denounced by John Stuart Mill. Common language usage also reflects this assumption. The man who loves a woman is said to 'possess' her – whereas the girl is merely taken in marriage. Legal codes often refer to this *a priori* distinction as being founded on natural differences or on historical tradition – which shows that they are uncertain whether it is rooted in nature or culture.

Madame Maria Verone (on the right), a
militant feminist, demonstrates against
the refusal to allow women the vote by
organising her own ballot boxes. French
women were finally given the vote in 1946.

Even in England, outside the sphere of influence of the Napoleonic code, married women are not treated as the equals of their husbands. The wife has no legal right to a share of her husband's earnings beyond household expenditure. If she is abandoned, her position is worse than in many other countries. Unless the mother takes a direct plea to the courts of law, she is in danger of losing custody of her children. In the United States, despite the Fourteenth Amendment guaranteeing equal legal protection to all, 'some distinctions remain of which the married woman is the most outstanding victim'. According to the Presidential Commission on the Status of Women, this results from the mixed legal heritage influencing American legislation: the British common law, to which were added certain French and Spanish precepts on marriage settlements. Thus in some states women on marriage lose some of their rights to control property, to work, to dispose of their earnings or to dispose of their possessions by will. In some states only the father has authority over the children.

The 'celibacy clause'. The Declaration on the Elimination of Discriminatory Practices against Women also recommended that a series of measures should be taken to assure the social and economic equality of women. These include the right to work, the right to education, the right to paid leave, retirement benefits, unemployment allowances and pensions identical with those of men, the right to family allowances like men, protection from dismissal in case of marriage and guaranteed maternity leave.

Apart from the priesthood, there is hardly an occupation from which a man may be dismissed upon marriage. On the other hand there still exists a 'celibacy clause' whereby an unmarried woman accepts that her contract of employment will automatically terminate if she marries. This practice has been declared illegal in Germany (although it still seems to be used there), in Italy and in France. A famous lawsuit was introduced and won by an air hostess against the airline Air France which asked air hostesses to give in their resignations if they married. In Britain a similar clause exists in some occupations (airlines, the diplomatic service, etc.), and is not illegal. The same applies to Belgium and the Netherlands. In the United States, Article 7 of the Civil Rights Act provides women with a legal instrument with which to fight any attempt to make them sign the 'celibacy clause'. The contribution of the Act to the emancipation of American women cannot be overestimated.

Allowances and pensions. The greatest inequalities between the sexes in this domain characterise the English-speaking countries. In Great Britain women make the same individual pension contributions as men, but they receive only sixpence per week for every nine pounds paid in, whereas men will receive sixpence for a contribution of seven pounds, ten shillings. This is the result of women's life expectations exceeding those of men. For the same reason, in the United States a widow will receive sixty-six dollars per month whereas her husband would have received seventy-six dollars per month in social security benefits, had he survived her. Often women do not have the same rights to unemployment benefit as men. In Great Britain the married woman worker who is sick receives benefits totalling less than the amount paid to the man or to the spinster (£3. 2. 0d. a week instead of £4. 10s. 0d.). There is of course no such disparity between married men and bachelors.

Maternity benefits. More attention has been paid to maternity benefits than to the independence or the economic rights of the mother. The times are fortunately over when the woman who had to earn a living was dismissed the moment she admitted to being pregnant or when the fact spoke for itself, or was compelled to work right up to the last moment and to resume immediately after childbirth. Two conventions of the ILO (1919 and 1952) have fixed minimal standards governing maternity benefits. These include six weeks, compulsory leave after childbirth and six weeks' optional leave before the expected date of birth, as well as security of tenure for pregnant women and payment of allowances during their leave. Out of the twenty-one member countries of the Organisation for Economic Co-operation and Development, all of which are at an advanced stage of development, only seven have signed the conventions: France, Germany, Greece, Italy, Luxemburg, Spain and Yugoslavia. Maternity leaves vary from country to country. Table 7:1 summarises these different provisions according to information provided by each of the governments concerned.

When the allowance paid to the mother is small, or assimilated to sickness benefits, this indicates that childbirth is considered as a disease by society, or perhaps as a regrettable occurrence which interrupts the work done by female employees, as would 'flu or a broken leg. Yet reproduction is ultimately a social activity, ensuring a future labour force.

All this shows the difficulties involved for women to adjust to a male-dominated world. To grant unpaid leave satisfies the conscience of legislators, but actually harms those they are trying to help, since most women – like men – must work for a living. Childbirth involves considerable outlays and therefore unpaid leave can be enjoyed by very few women. The others do not avail themselves of this opportunity. In France, where during permitted leave of absence half of the wages are received, more than three million days of maternity leave are annually given up, because the women entitled to them do not want to lose the other half of their earnings. Economists, administrators and employers object to women's desire to have their cake and eat it, to reproduce and to go on earning, to be students and workers without modifying their female role. This desire is considered unrealistic, but in fact the only way to be realistic in the world of work is to be a man. Realism for a woman only involves the acceptance of additional handicaps of an economic, psychological and physiological nature. The most realistic attitude may consist in facing up to this uncomfortable and guilt-provoking situation.

Maternity leave no longer has to be fought for. It is given willingly by the majority of governments, even if the benefits are

Table 7:1 Maternity leave and benefits in sixteen countries

Country	Pre-natal leave	Post-natal leave	Allowances excluding premium paid at birth
Austria	No provision	10 weeks or longer	Allowances
Canada	Variation from province to province Often no fixed arrangements		Leave with pay rare
Denmark	Manual work – no provision. Non manual work – 3-5 months	Manual work – 4 weeks Non manual work – 3-5 months	50 per cent of earnings
Eire	6 weeks	6 weeks	?
France	6 weeks	8 weeks	50 per cent of earnings plus employers' contributions
Federal Germany	6 weeks	6 weeks	Partial social security benefits
Greece	6 weeks	6 weeks	?
Italy	Obligatory leave 6, 8 or 12 weeks according to job	8 weeks	Benefits
Netherlands	Nothing or 2 weeks	6 or 8 weeks	Variable
Norway	Overall leave up to 6 weeks	4 weeks	?
Spain	6 weeks	6 weeks	?
Sweden	No compulsory leave Unpaid leave – 25 weeks	Maximum possible	Allowances approx. 30 per cent of wages
Switzerland	No provision	6 to 8 weeks	Variable
UK	No general regulation		Variable
USA	No general regulation		Allowances rare
Yugoslavia	6 weeks	9 weeks	Social benefits

215

lower than the minimum fixed by the ILO. Difficulties are postponed to a later stage and criticism begins when the mother is first absent from work because her child is sick. Childbirth for governments and husbands alike is an almost sacred period, a truce during which all conspire to look after the women. But this emotional reaction is of short duration; soon all is as before, even for the young mother overloaded with work, without nursery facilities, household help or family aid. Indeed, many women have no other rest in their lives than the week of relaxation after childbirth.

The Convention on the Political Rights of Women was adopted by the General Assembly of the United Nations in 1952. In essence it gave women equal rights with men to vote at all elections, to be eligible for all elected public bodies established by national legislation, and to occupy any public posts or offices created by such legislation. No form of discrimination should exclude women from any of these political activities. By 1964 only forty-two member States had ratified this convention, though many of these made reservations to Article 3 'access to public office'. It is easier to grant women the right to vote and to stand for election than to accept their presence in administrative posts.

In order to encourage further signatories, the United Nations Secretariat organised several round table conferences in which regional experts compared views on this issue. These were held at Ulan Bator (for Asia), Bangkok (for South-East Asia), Bogota (for Latin America) and Addis Ababa (for Africa). A round table on the participation of women in local government was also held in Hungary.

'Women Figureheads'

Instead of summarising the results of this work in terms of the usual comments on the effects of male prejudice and the even greater influence of female prejudice, let us quote the intervention of Marguerite Thibert in an international seminar on the participation of women in public life. Having been attached to the International Labour Office for many years, having studied the status of women since the beginning of the century in all parts of the world, Marguerite Thibert summarised her experiences in the following statement:

Without wishing to hurt anyone's feelings, one may say that these results are fairly disappointing. Official documents may be quoted in evidence of this. Despite the climate of diplomatic reserve which prevails in these meetings where participants, if not actually representing their countries in the strict sense of the term, are at least experts designated by their respective governments, one can find in the reports of the Commision on the Status of Women many disenchanted comments.

Mrs Gandhi in New Delhi, 1967.
Women rulers were once accepted
only as hereditary monarchs.

At this point it would be easy to cite the evidence for the defence by simply reading out the list of successful women which can be found in many women's magazines. As evidence of progress one could say that Miss X and Mrs Y have been appointed secretaries of state and congratulate them on their well-earned promotion. However, while not wishing to detract from the merits of the few, one should not forget that they remain the exception which proves the rule. This poses a problem which Madame Thibert analyses as follows:

In studying the situation in detail, I fear one discovers numerous cases of a purely symbolic form of female promotion which I can only consider deplorable in its effects, namely the appointment of 'women figureheads' to posts of responsibility. By this phrase I mean to indicate the appointment of a woman to an important post simply as a sop to current public opinion in favour of equality between the sexes, but without any intention of repeating this gesture. In the past, regulations have sometimes legalised this trick by making a minimum female quota obligatory in certain administrative bodies.

These figureheads have never helped to open the door to other women, but rather to close it more firmly behind themselves, since the minimum quota of women has tended to be regarded as the maximum number possible. This method which consists in granting one woman a privilege may destroy female solidarity. A vain woman will take pride in this exceptional promotion, a reasonable woman can only feel uneasy in such a situation. She is almost compelled to adopt the attitudes of her male counterparts, since it requires a large influx of new elements into a previously closed sphere for change to take place.

Neutralising the forces of change

The advancement of women in public life is thus shown in its true light. There have always been exceptional women in each generation under all regimes, from Theodora to Indira Gandhi: such women as Eleanor of Aquitaine, Joan of Arc, Elizabeth I and Catherine of Russia and so many others, not to mention the female professors of law in the eleventh century, founders of religious orders like Saint Teresa, educational reformers and revolutionaries. It would appear that each generation of women

counts among its members a number of innovating individuals who are often in 'anomic' situations (to use Durkheim's term). They are neither normal nor abnormal, but often tend to be non-conformist and are thus differentiated from the mass. They tend to stand out from their contemporaries and have often been considered as heretics or even put to death for their lack of orthodoxy. Nowadays they are often turned into female figureheads, a tiny minority whose existence testifies to egalitarian values, but which is made innocuous by becoming part of the system. Indeed the art of social control is to integrate even deviants and innovators in order to neutralise their influence.

A very small percentage of women is tolerated as a permissible variation from the norm so as not to bring into question the prevailing situation. Such gifted women, far from being abnormal, are merely confronted by a world in which it is difficult for them to exercise their ability to act or to think, a world which is hostile to their ideas. Like Antigone, they are more aware of the need for change because they suffer more than their contemporaries from

present constraints. In present-day society such women are promptly cut down to size by public opinion, which dismisses them as 'unfeminine', therefore 'butch' and 'abnormal'. They are treated with condescending indulgence. After all they are few in number and there is always the consoling adage to fall back on that 'A career woman cannot be happy since professional success for a woman is only making the best of a bad deal' – a saying which is popular with those who have failed and who may not be happy for all that. Alternatively people say 'She may be outstanding but she is not what I call a woman'. This implies that a woman is defined by her inability to succeed and lead rather than by physiology or psychology.

Exceptional women tend to stimulate change. However, one wonders how far these two or three per cent of women welcomed into positions of authority may use their gifts in the interest of all women or whether their teeth have already been drawn. Often they are considered as the representatives of women without having meant to be so, and they are content to secure a position for

Valentina Nikolayeva Tereshkova,
a woman 'figurehead' and a symbol
of female courage.

221

themselves rather than try to open the door for others to follow them. Even for those seeking to help other women the situation is difficult. First, they are a minority group and it is enough to imagine the lack of impact two per cent of men would have in a female gathering to understand the intrinsic weakness of minorities. I have often witnessed the effect that being a small minority among women has on men in all kinds of circumstances and in various countries; they are unfailingly silent and intimidated.

Secondly, individuals who have enough intelligence and vitality to be outstanding accept the fact that they differ from others – although different is not synonymous with abnormal. It is expected of 'women figureheads' that their oddity (in being both women and ministers) will lead them to become like their male colleagues in performing the same duties. Their success in other words consists in being accepted as 'a man like any other' and in not being treated any longer like a woman. They are not expected to bring too many women in their wake, but to remain 'charming exceptions' to a rigidly enforced rule. Since the 'woman figurehead' is accepted only because she is different from other women, she is gradually made to dissociate herself from them. She is meant to work alongside men rather than for women. If she sees herself as the spearhead of a mass of underprivileged women, she is no longer abiding by the rules of the game.

Finally, whether they are women of straw or strong personalities, it is always difficult for women who make up less than ten or even five per cent of an assembly to be anything more than symbols. While there have certainly been exceptionally able women representatives, large-scale change requires that pressure from the grass-roots should increase and many more women continue their slow progress up the occupational ladder. However, this stage of advancement is still remote, and current statistics give no grounds for undue optimism.

Women's decreasing political power

Great Britain, the country with the biggest suffragette movement, presents a curious record of victories achieved by women. English women complain bitterly about the weakness of their political representation and in so far as they restrict themselves to criticising parliament, one can understand their point of view. Between 1951 and 1964 women constituted only five per cent of prospective Conservative MPS and seven per cent of Labour Party candidates. Furthermore, the constituencies fought by them tended to be lost causes. According to Austin Ranney in *Pathways to Parliament*, in the 1967 elections nineteen women successfully contested seats for Labour, thus providing 5·5 per cent of MPs in the governing party. On the other hand, seven women gained seats for the Conservative party, thus representing 2·8 per cent of the opposition. Female representation in the post-election parliament equalled 4·1 per cent of all MPS, to which one should add a further female Scottish Nationalist candidate successful in the by-election of November 1967 and one female MP from Northern Ireland elected in 1969. Women in the House of Commons therefore occupied less than five per cent of parliamentary seats. However, they have achieved a disproportionately large share of governmental posts (ten women held ministerial posts at the time of writing). Moreover, women hold a greater number of seats in local government than they do in the majority of other countries, excluding the People's Democracies. Over the whole of the British Isles they represent twelve per cent of the membership of borough and county councils. In London they made up twenty-one per cent of members on the Metropolitan Borough Council and twenty-eight per cent of the old London County Council. However, in 1967 they accounted for only seventeen per cent of the Greater London Council.

This share in local government is a great step forward, but falls short of being a complete success, since women have never accounted for more than a quarter of any council and never exceeded twelve per cent for the whole country. Despite this, local government is often referred to as woman-ridden – a strange exaggeration in a country famous for its understatements. Since twelve per cent of local representatives are female, eighty-eight per cent must be male, and the fact that they feel threatened is merely one example of the resistance put up by men when women cease to be figureheads and become significant individuals. For all their personality, technical competence and fighting spirit, one can imagine the difficulties met by women in British politics, in a country where the treatment of their sex is in some respects less egalitarian than in continental Europe.

French women, who yearly make a greater and greater assault on the universities and increasingly attain the prestige that positions in the higher Civil Service confer, have had an insignificant impact on national politics. Their very small contribution under the Fourth Republic, forty female deputies out of 630 in 1946, i.e., 6·4 per cent of seats, was further narrowed in the Gaullist Fifth Republic. Thus there were only eleven female deputies out of 487 in 1967, a drop to 2·3 per cent and the mounting tide of Gaullist votes caused three women deputies of the left and the extreme left to lose their seats in the 1968 election. Traditionally, many more female candidates have stood for election on behalf of left-wing groups, particularly in the Communist Party, than for centre or right-wing ones. A similar reduction in the number of seats occupied by women occurred in the Senate after 1958 (from eleven to five female senators). Again the percentage of women holding seats on the municipal councils fell from a ratio of one woman to thirty-two men in 1947 to one to forty-one in 1965. Thus the participation of women was 2·4 per cent of the total at municipal level, a proportion which later reached three per cent. Only the number of female mayors has steadily increased, from 260 in 1947 to 300 in 1953, to 381 in 1960 and recently to over 400. But unless municipal councils include many women, these numbers are likely to shrink in the future. In France there is no doubt that anti-feminism is strongest in politics and among politicians, both openly and

clothed in gallant compliments and uninhibited jokes. Conceivably French women think that abandoning the political arena to men is a fair price for retaining good relations between the sexes. These traditional and emotional reactions should be contrasted with historical facts. French women played an extremely important part in the Resistance, but their activities took place under cover of secrecy. Clearly women are more ready to risk their lives than to risk public ridicule. After the Liberation, the first elections returned many former Resistance members, including a number of women, and this trend could have been expected to increase in future years. Instead political tradition reasserted itself, with its emphasis on publicity, its prize-fighting and its snares. Women drew back. Furthermore, the French electorate was no longer expected after the war to vote for a group, but for individuals. Whereas men had previously accepted the entry of one or two women on the lists of candidates as a harmless concession, it was quite a different decision to allow one women to represent a party as sole candidate for the constituency. For woman also, the new form of voting presented disadvantages, accentuating as it did public performance and exposure to public accusations of being

First meeting of the Greater London Council, 1967.
Women are comparatively well represented on
this council (seventeen per cent as opposed to
under five per cent of women MPs in parliament).

225

unfeminine. Immediately too a whole new series of slogans was coined, such as 'Women draw fewer votes than men', although this is quite unproven. English surveys on this topic have shown that for the Labour and Liberal voters there is no significant difference in attitudes to male and female candidates, whereas among Conservative supporters only one per cent stated their unwillingness to vote for a woman. An alternative and more pernicious slogan is the well-known saying 'Women will not vote for other women', meaning that there is no solidarity between them. This allegation is quite groundless, as the author has found in a study (albeit a small-scale one). Further investigations should be conducted to substantiate this result.

Most of the points made about France are also true for Italy, where the number of female deputies has been decreasing with each successive election. However the *apertura a sinistra* has halted this trend. Indeed in Italy as in other countries women are mainly elected by left-wing votes. It should also be noted that Italian women are politically more active than is generally believed abroad or even in their own country. This may be due to the striking contrast between their archaic position in Italian society and the rapid social change caused in the last ten years by the increase in economic prosperity. For instance the ban on divorce is strongly resented by many women. In the young generation the change of attitudes is especially striking.

In the Italian parliament the number of female deputies steadily decreased between 1945 and 1960, but a slight increase took place in 1963. The first post-war parliament counted forty-five women (eight per cent of its total membership), the second, thirty-four (seven per cent), the third, twenty-five (four per cent) and the fourth, twenty-seven (4·5 per cent). In municipal and provincial councils women's participation is even lower, since they represent only 1·5 per cent of members. In the Italian parliament there are more women both in absolute numbers and as a proportion of the total than in the British, the French and the American assemblies, but this is not backed up by a strong body of female councillors

A French woman mayor performing
the marriage ceremony.

at local level which could provide and train future candidates for national elections. Those who have been elected thus appear to be an active and isolated minority rather than a spearhead.

In this respect the United States is even more backward than Italy, although Latin and Catholic traditions are generally held to be adverse to women's progress. As the Kennedy Commission on the Status of Women noted, the weakness of female representation in political life is 'a fact which astonishes the visitor from abroad on arrival in America'. The allegedly matriarchal society has always had a poor record of female participation in politics. Before the last elections, there were only two women senators as against one hundred men, and eleven women out of a total of 435 in the House of Representatives. Out of 307 federal judges, only two are women. Under the last three administrations (one Republican and two Democrat), the Federal Government counted only 2·4 per cent of women officials. Before the last elections women held 234 seats out of 7,700 in state parliaments i.e., three per cent of all seats. 'The low percentage of women in public life reflects the small proportion of women at the top of the professions which are the most usual channels into politics and state offices', according to American experts. It is also pointed out that women lack the popular appeal needed to make a political career, they lack 'showmanship' – an expression which aptly conveys the requirements of American politics. On the other hand one should not forget the very high degree of participation by American women in private voluntary associations which pursue civic aims and often have an important influence on local politics. One of their organisers referred to these volunteers as 'a force for change', but this force should surely apply itself to political life on a national scale.

In the great majority of developed countries, women cast proportionally as many votes as men; being the more numerous sex, they tend to cast a majority of votes. Furthermore they do not abstain more often than men, except in the United States, where, particularly in the south, they tend to be less conscientious in having their names entered on the electoral register. Many power-

American women display a natural tendency to form into groups, from powerful women's organisations to small informal gatherings. Shown here is a 'baby shower' where the mother-to-be is showered with presents.

ful associations of women in fact attempt to influence voters, especially female voters, to exercise their electoral rights. They do so with considerable determination in strict neutrality, merely supporting the view that the use of the vote is a civic duty. However, despite the trouble and the money spent on these efforts, the rate of female voting in the United States remains lower than in other countries where female abstention is only twenty or even ten per cent, without any encouragement to vote.

It may be presumptuous to venture an opinion on a subject so well-documented as that of the American woman, but it really seems that the famous American matriarchy is a myth perpetuated in comic strips and on psychoanalysts' couches. For all their free ways, their independence, their activity and their efficiency, American women seem to lag further behind men in economic, professional, academic and political life (in all the spheres power is defined by) than the women of other countries at whom the accusation of matriarchy has never been levelled. All the stories about husbands in aprons doing the washing up and minding the children are really red herrings. They cannot account for the myth of women's power spread by fiction, movies and cartoons. It is precisely women's exclusion from administrative, economic and political leadership which results in the popular assertion that they are a power behind the scenes. This is an unexpected consequence of the segregation of male and female roles, which also results in the concept of 'togetherness', intended to transcend barriers between the sexes. One aspect of 'togetherness' is that the wife of an elected representative should feel that she too has been elected. It is certainly true that the wife of a politician has a role to play in politics and is an important element in her husband's success or failure. But who is to believe that there is no difference between this gentle creature who backs up her husband and decorates his publicity campaign, and the female candidate running her own campaign, assuming full responsibility for her acts and beliefs, and finally winning a seat for herself? The complex structure of marital mythology concocted by psychoanalysts, psycho-

logists and journalists is not very satisfying as a substitute for female equality. Nor can background influence ever compare with direct participation. More and more young American women are coming to recognise this and they are no less feminine for it.

German women, although they are renowned for their discipline and for their submissiveness to masculine decisions, are proportionately more numerous among Bundestag members than their English, Italian, French and American counterparts in the parliaments of those countries. In the Netherlands, women accounted for one per cent of the membership of provincial assemblies and two per cent of municipal councils in 1960 (according to UNESCO data). In Belgium there were 526 women in municipal assemblies out of 30,000 members, i.e., about 1·75 per cent.

Political education

The problem of female representation has a double aspect: on the one hand, every woman elected is one who in political terms has educated herself, who has learnt that 'politics is the art of the possible' and that all major decisions are ultimately due to it. On the other hand, she must educate female voters in her turn and by her very existence. This process can only be called successful if there is an increase, however slight, in the percentage of women elected. It is only then that the female politician will see her prestige rise in society and that the political education of women voters, members of voluntary associations and local representatives will improve.

In western Europe, this stage seems to have been reached only by Sweden (and to some extent by Finland), since the Swedish national election has returned a steadily increasing number of women, reaching fifteen per cent of the membership of all elected assemblies. If the lofty statements on equality between the sexes which form the preamble of so many national constitutions are to have any meaning, this can only be through their translation into political equality and the education indispensable for equality of political opportunity.

The more this problem is studied, the more difficult its interpretation becomes. Thus, it seems untrue to assert that a correlation exists between the number of women who have quietly secured educational diplomas and professional status and the number of female representatives in elected assemblies. The French experience is a case in point, since female advancement in higher education and in occupational life has been considerable, while women's political participation has not proceeded apace. It appears that a very important variable determining the level of female representation is the nature of the political regime. Generally one finds that it is the socialist parties and, to an even greater extent, the more extreme left-wing parties which are more prepared to designate women as potential candidates than conservative parties are, even though the numbers involved in both cases are small. The trend is certainly paradoxical in view of the fact that the parties which nominate most women suffer most from the female tendency to vote conservative. However, this alleged propensity of female voters is more apparent than real. In many countries, it can be explained by the fact that the suffrage only became universal after the Second World War. Those women who are today aged forty-five or over were brought up in the belief that politics was not for them, since they did not have the vote. The younger generations aged between twenty-one and thirty-five are the only women who should be compared with their male contemporaries. In fact according to the public opinion polls conducted before various national elections, their choices are not widely different from those of men. It is only the mass of older women who have a more conservative attitude than the men of the same age.

It should also be noted that it is precisely in developing countries, and particularly in those with strong traditions of segregation between the sexes, that a few women have made spectacular political careers by the standards of western democracies. The only female head of state, Indira Gandhi, belongs to a nation where for centuries there were traditions of female impurity and female segregation. In the East, as well as in Africa, the post-colonial period has witnessed the political advancement of women, particularly in Vietnam and in People's China.

This leads to the whole question of female participation in the political life of communist countries. In the Soviet Union the number of women elected is strikingly greater than elsewhere – forty-three per cent at the local level and twenty-nine per cent at the national level. In local government, this obviously corresponds to a new development, particularly in the traditionally Moslem regions where women used to be strictly isolated and today are governing provinces and even representing men. However, one could not argue seriously that political power has ever ceased to be concentrated in the hands of a few leaders, all of whom have been men. One should be cautious in assessing the Soviet Union: women have gained a share in management, but not in power, nor in decision making.

In conclusion, one must admit that in a world fraught with danger, in which armaments absorb such a large part of national budgets, in which conflicts are always breaking out and always threatening to escalate, women – although they wish for peace – have not fully done their duty in opposing war. They have always preferred to shed tears than to work realistically and continuously in the cause of peace. They should not forget that they are all too often to blame for overpopulation. They are frequently unaware of and sometimes resigned to their role in adding to the world's starving and illiterate masses. It is not therefore a simple issue of political rights, but of duties which women must assume if they truly mean that they want peace and welfare for all and that they oppose aggressive imperialism and total power.

9 The church

Women have played a great part, either directly or indirectly in the troubled life of the churches in recent years, and especially in that of the Catholic church. A visitor from another planet would find it paradoxical that while the majority of church-goers are women, religious doctrines certainly do not value the female sex very highly, or at least have been misinterpreted over the centuries to give women a subordinate role in religious practices. They have been debarred from conducting religious services and administering the sacraments. A growing number of them now rejects the self-effacement involved in this definition of their religious role. In the Catholic church for instance, twentieth-century women have lost all the importance they possessed in the Middle Ages and more-over have become increasingly aware of the divide separating their real life, in marriage, the family and society, from that which the church seeks to impose. Scientific and medical progress which has slowly transformed the pattern of daily life, even to the extent of modifying the process of growth and ageing, does not seem to have been assimilated into the church's doctrines on women's duties. While women have been more reticent than men in the great debate about the future of Catholicism, it is significant that for the first time some female representatives should have attended the Vatican Council. Even female orders, traditionally detached from the world, are increasingly involved in controversy about the role of nuns and the nature of their calling.

In the Protestant churches, less rigid because less hierarchical in structure, women have been accepted in the ministry for the first time, thus becoming the equals of men in the clergy. In Germany, Sweden and France, the transition has been smooth and they are now accepted by their congregations. It is to be expected that the churches will increasingly draw on female clergy, as the religious calling declines steadily among men.

The awakening of women's minds, this departure from their former passive obedience (or at least the pretence of it) has been particularly significant in relation to the thorny question of family planning. While this is not the place to enter into a detailed discus-

A Swedish woman minister baptises a child.

sion of the theological views propounded in an extraordinarily abundant literature, it should be stressed that planned parenthood has been claimed by the masses of women in all countries. Everywhere women themselves have initiated family planning organisations and pressed for medical research and political decisions to further birth control. Despite the fact that most discoveries and most legislative acts bear the name of a man, it must not be overlooked that the idea of family planning was invented by women who sought the first solutions for its implementation. Nor should the names of pioneers such as Marie Stopes in England and Margaret Sanger in the United States be forgotten.

The reaction of women to the encyclical *Humanae Vitae* has been a striking one. While men commented at length using all the available mass media, women made few public statements. Doubtless many submitted in silence. Others, equally silent, have rebelled in deed, if not in words. In the weeks following the publication of the encyclical, birth control clinics in Catholic countries were inundated by new patients from Catholic families, while chemists saw their stock of contraceptive preparations dwindle in countries where these clinics were not allowed. Such truths cannot remain hidden in the future.

In the current dilemma of the Catholic church women are deeply involved. On the one hand, convents, orders and religious associations no longer conform to the traditional pattern or appearance of female reticence and humility, but question many basic assumptions. On the other, the concept of womanhood is being re-examined and traditional theological views are increasingly changed and challenged as crude and archaic. The deep distrust of women, held to be sinful creatures in need of authority, is no longer accepted by leading theologians (some of whom are now women) and is increasingly contested by the mass of churchgoers. It is becoming more and more evident that a couple cannot attain fulfilment, even of a spiritual or mystical kind, if constrained by a pattern of domination and submission, but only if a recognition of freedom and similar identity exists between the partners. The com-

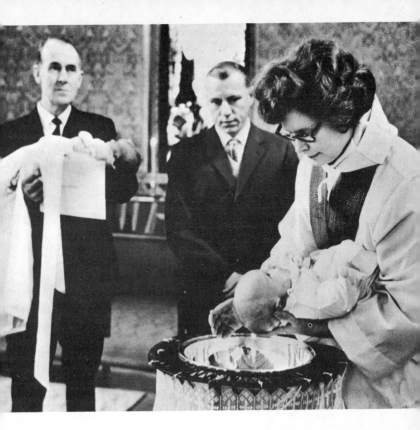

plex sphere of sexual life is also being studied and is proving a
difficult task, since male sexual needs, even the most deviant, are
better known and more widely accepted by the church than female
ones. For example the church has never considered frigidity in
women as abnormal.

The stimulus to deal with such problems can be found in the
modern woman's hedonistic outlook, in her quest for pleasure and
happiness. To many minds this is a disturbing attitude and fears
about women tend to outweigh hopes. Female freedom always
seems fraught with dangers rather than rich possibilities. It may
seem strange that at a time when the abandoning of celibacy for
the Catholic clergy is talked of as probable, there is hardly any
reference to what priests' wives might or would be. It is clearly

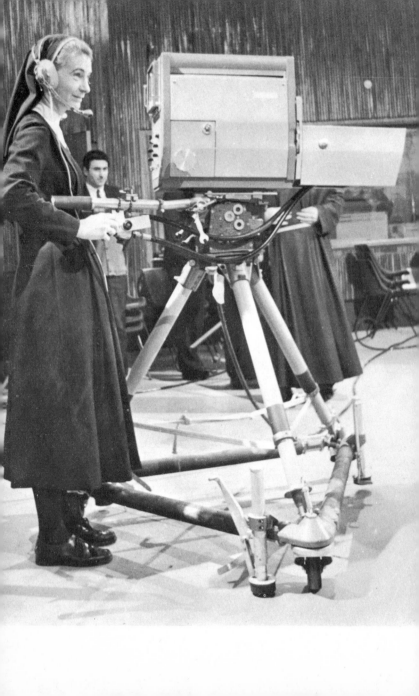

Nuns today seek to take a more active part in the modern world. This nun is taking a training course at the Catholic Radio and Television Centre near London.

felt that their existence would only be accepted by the church as a necessary evil, a surrender to temptation rather than a call for useful helpmates. Meanwhile the wives of Protestant ministers remain silent, not liking to expose the weakness of their position.

It is among lay believers more than among the clergy that a great change is taking place and traditional conceptions of woman, defined either as weak and impure or as meek and submissive to the authority of her husband, are giving way to a new image. Little by little men are discovering in their wives what the female protestant theologian, F. Dumas, has called their 'other likeness' – the emphasis being on identity rather than on difference.

Many interesting aspects of women's life in the modern world have of necessity been left aside. Those issues which can be compared cross-culturally have been stressed, but such an approach has its limitations as, for example, to discuss part-time work in a few pages would be impossible. The problem is of such complexity and so different in nature from country to country that one must study it at national level rather than gloss over important variations to arrive at superficial conclusions.

Maternal and paternal roles

Similarly, there has been little discussion of the subject of woman's maternal role, since it has been thoroughly explored elsewhere and some consensus has been reached. It should not be forgotten, however, that this role has never been more important, since modern times are the culmination of a historical trend which has increasingly widened its scope. In the past women were not responsible for the education of boys, and had little to say in the education of girls. At the end of the eighteenth century mothers began to assume wider responsibilities for the socialisation of their children, though the fathers remained in control. The concurrent processes of industrialisation, urbanisation and bureaucratisation absorbed so many men on the labour market that authority over their children's upbringing was relinquished to their wives. This new role allocation is now so firmly established that to many women it seems rooted both in nature and history. Thus it appears to them perfectly normal that mothers should deal with pocket money and homework as part of their undivided responsibility for child-rearing. Today socialisation is a mother-dominated process, though this has not always been so in history and, it is to be hoped, will not remain so much longer. There is a growing disquiet about the eclipse of the paternal role. Millions of children are constantly surrounded by women: in the home, in the neighbourhood, at primary school where form teachers, the school medical worker and the rest of the teaching staff tend to be female. As teaching has ceased to be a male preserve, women have acquired responsi-

bilities in formal education as well as in informal socialisation. Although they are proud of this new role, the balance between the sexes should be restored, for children need male, as well as female, educators, and the father's presence is as necessary as that of the mother. While mothers increasingly need to find interests outside the home and to play a wider role in local and national life, men, for their part, need to rediscover their domestic role, responsibilities and power of decision-making, giving up their total absorption in professional life which for some has meant a withdrawal from their family and even a decline in emotional involvement.

If more women worked, this might result in shorter working hours for all, and might thus be to the advantage of both sexes.

Most women spend their lives in a closed
world of children and household chores.

241

Men would have more time for family life and for leisure time
activities than they can afford at present. Women would cease to
be torn between different forms of second best: either to remain
at home and let their horizons shrink, particularly after the children
have grown up, or do two jobs at once, or to accept the compromise of part-time work where both the pay and the duties will
be less satisfying.

The reappraisal of parental roles has already started. It is not
only the Victorian family which is dead, but also the family of the
period between the 'thirties and the 'sixties, in which the father
was the only breadwinner and the mother his domestic bursar.
This type in which the mother's role was dominant corresponded
to a transition between the patriarchal model of early industrial
societies and the pattern towards which our highly developed
urbanised societies are moving. In the world of tomorrow parental
roles will presumably cease to be specialised. The parental couple
whose present roles conflict and yet who complement each other
(this has never more clearly been described than in Freudian
psychology) will share rather than divide responsibilities in future.
In the words of the Swedish author Edmund Dahlström:

> The idea of women's two roles [to quote the title of the famous work by
> Viola Klein and Alva Myrdal] is no longer tenable. One can no longer
> speak of a male and of a female role, but only of a human role, common to
> both sexes and including the upbringing of children.

Household chores

This happy stage cannot be reached, however, unless housework is
reorganised on a rational basis. The work of the housewife is less
and less concerned with production, but compels her to waste a
tremendous amount of time on repetitive and uninteresting tasks.
Some of these are certainly creative and demand intelligence –
cooking, for instance, is more than giving enough to eat, decorating
the house is more than making it habitable, and dressing well is
more than clothing one's body. All these minor art forms add up
to a way of life in which all can express their personalities, their

gifts, their tastes and their cultural heritage. But can the same be said of dusting, or washing up, or cleaning utensils again and again? No one could call these jobs constructive. Rather than share them with men, it would be better to invent time-saving methods to reduce the billions of hours wasted every year on such unproductive work. In the words of the poet, women's lives are dedicated to 'travaux ennuyeux et faciles' (chores which are dull and easy). The time for poetic commiseration is past; the moment for practical solutions is upon us, but hardly any progress has yet been made towards eliminating this negative side of housework which is devoid of creative aspects and which gives satisfaction to no one. Increase in home appliances has saved effort, but not time. As Alva Myrdal says, little has been done to devise collective solutions for household chores. Progress in the organisation of day nurseries is slow, yet while it is now a well-established fact that the presence of the mother is necessary to her child, it is certainly not true that she must be present twenty-four hours out of twenty-four.

Social provisions of this kind will not be made without strong pressure from women. As discussions with experts in different countries have shown, these problems do not interest modern administrators. Those who could devise or introduce time- or labour-saving solutions do not care, since they themselves never have to do housework or look after babies. They tend to invoke the cost of such provisions and above all their non-profit-making character. By extension of this argument one wonders on what grounds non-profit-making services such as hospitals, public gardens, viaducts or motorways are justified. Their contribution to the economy is indirect in all cases. Moreover, an indirect profit could be derived from services which freed women for wider participation in society. In addition the education given to girls in all countries would pay dividends instead of yielding nothing, as in the case of thousands of secondary school leavers who spend half their life on housework instead of using their qualifications. However, we are far from having reached that stage. Even Lenin

did not succeed in releasing women from the kitchen sink. The main obstacle to progress remains the fear of making women's life too similar to that of men. While the condition of women may be changing constantly, it still remains inferior to or less advanced than that of men.

Theoretical problems

The distance between the condition of women and that of men in society has been attributed to a difference in their nature and has therefore been construed as both logical and final. Obviously there are some undeniable differences in terms of anatomy and physical strength (though women compensate for their weakness by being more resistant to infection). However, there are no clearly cut lines dividing the sexes in this respect, and women who work in the fields make greater physical efforts than many male clerks. More important perhaps are differences in hormone composition. Endocrinologists have shown that while hormones greatly influence behaviour, the demarcation line between the sexes is not firmly drawn. There is no sharp contrast in this respect, and women with an excess of female hormones can be as energetic and enterprising as the men who have the greatest concentration of testosterone. The implications of the difference between male and female chromosomic structure have not been so fully explored. This is in fact a very clear-cut and unchanging difference. For the time being it is only known that the last pair of chromosomes (xx for women and xy for men) determines sex, but the meaning of this is not fully grasped, nor is the exact contribution of this chromosomic composition to psychological male and female make-up. We are only beginning to detect the consequences of certain abnormal chromosome formulae (in some cases the last xy pair is replaced by a trio xxy or xyy) which seem to correspond to certain behavioural differences. This type of study, though only in its infancy, does show that despite such anomalies men and women are usually differentiated by the composition of their last pair of chromosomes. Genetic differences may have determinant consequences for sexual behaviour and may ultimately lead to a modification of historical and sociological explanations of sex typing. Genetics may prove that Simone de Beauvoir was wrong in writing 'One is not born a woman, one becomes a woman'.

However, genetical explanations are clearly insufficient to account for differences between the sexes which cannot be reduced to disparities in physical and mental make-up, but which consist in unsychronised rates of development. It is impossible to explain by reference to anatomical or physiological determinism how women today can be doctors, professors of mathematics or aeroplane pilots, but only after men have reached those levels, just as there is a cultural lag between underdeveloped and developed countries. This historical gap between the achievements of the sexes cannot be accounted for by innate differences in ability. It would be more accurate to say that the male group, having early taken the lead and placed itself in positions of power, has now the authority to define which activities carry prestige and which do not, which deserve a high remuneration and which do not, making definitions so as to conserve their advantage. They can even impose the type of advancement they will allow women to have, in rather the same way that industrialised countries influence the rate of modernisation of the underdeveloped countries. We have seen how in educational and occupational terms there are millions of examples showing that two parallel ladders have been erected for men and for women.

The differential rates of national development accentuate the lack of uniformity in the condition of women throughout the world. At the present time there are women living who are intellectually and technologically much more advanced than the men from other nations. If women from the Soviet Union and men from Upper Volta were made to live in the same country, the females through their superior knowledge would certainly dominate the males, whose great physical strength would not compensate for their ignorance. Yet these advanced women and primitive men people the world today. Unfortunately the chance has never arisen to test whether the cultural lag between the sexes could be reversed, since in all societies, rich or poor, industrialised or underdeveloped, men lead the way. Even among American Negroes, where women tend to be more educated than men, their wages are lower. It seems that the condition of women can only be analysed by reference to that of men in any society and at any time in history.

Periodically there is an increase or a decrease in the degree of equality between the sexes in the sphere of ideological beliefs, economic structure or social condition. This means that the two sexes do not develop along strictly parallel lines, since the distance separating them has varied over time. Discontinuity in this evolution is often initiated by spurts of progress limited to men, which are more or less rapidly followed by female demands for, and gradual achievement of, a comparable status. Many examples of such processes of widening and narrowing the distance between the sexes can be traced in history. Earlier in the text mention has been made of the suffragettes, a small female élite often ignored by public opinion and ridiculed by many people of both sexes. This movement eventually allowed women to make up for some of the neglect in which they were held during the time that men improved their status by social conflict in the nineteenth century. It is such minority groups of feminists who, often in a climate of general disapproval, achieve readjustment which then becomes the socially accepted norm.

Nevertheless, to overstress the analogies between women and underdeveloped countries, colonised or achieving independence, would be misleading. While it is certainly true that the mass of women are dominated, and to a large extent exploited, by the male sex, the situation is not explosive and, as far as one can see, never will be. Fortunately it seems clear that, outside mythology, erotic fantasy and fiction and of course the real life of bickering couples, there will never be a direct confrontation between the sexes. This is because women, unlike a colonised nation, an under-privileged race or people, or an exploited social class, do not form a group which can unite and fight for independence. Within the web of society, interdependent relationships between the sexes minimise the potential conflict between them. Ties of affection between wives and husbands, mothers and sons, sisters and brothers, girl and boy friends cut across relationships of domination and submission. Recourse to violence, implying as it does the negation of these bonds and social regrouping by sex, is quite unthinkable. Women do not even consider it and would not dream of dissociating themselves from their own men. The strategy of revolution and political tactics is not applicable in this case. This fact escapes many men who think that, since nothing would be easier than for women to revolt if their hearts were in it, their quiescence is evidence of slavish submission. Such political parallels are crude and superficial.

If revolutionary change is excluded, this does not mean that rapid non-violent reform is impossible. Such change might even occur without the participation or involvement of women themselves, simply because certain aspects of modern life favour them by reducing some of their natural disadvantages or by promoting the values traditionally associated with their sex.

Thus, for instance, it appears that recent medical discoveries now allow women to control their reproductive functions; further progress in this respect may be expected. Moreover, as we have seen, their expectation of life has been increased and the phases into which it is divided have become more akin to those of men. Their outlook, in which acceptance or resignation predominated for thousands of years while they were slaves to their own fertility, has gradually become imbued with the characteristics of any moral philosophy – judgment, choice and responsibility. By acquiring more education, a greater mastery over their destiny and increased chances of sexual fulfilment, women are becoming more like men. However, it would be a mistake to assume that economic and political change will follow automatically. Power is still a male preserve and one which will be jealously guarded from female intrusion in both the economic and governmental domain. The new egalitarian ideology propagated by the international organisations will only permit a gradual correction of the most blatant forms of discrimination against women.

The unwitting revenge of women in the world of today is that they are essential to the solution of all its great political problems. Overpopulation, starvation, underdevelopment, illiteracy – all of these issues can only be solved with the assistance of women. The most powerful political leaders cannot impose policies of population control, of economic development and educational expansion without the positive contribution of women. Without this, politicians have only the power to destroy, not to create.

Select bibliography

This bibliography does not attempt to do more than provide a brief guide to the subject of female sociology. Figures and statistics in the text are taken from the national statistical institutes, UNO, UNESCO, EEC, OECD, ILO, etc. Asterisks refer to paperback editions.

Arana, Amelia, *Cuadernos por el Dialogo*, June 1966 (special issue on Spanish women), Madrid.

Beauvoir, Simone de, *Le deuxieme sexe*, Paris, 1949; *The Second Sex*, London, 1962, trans. H. M. Paishley.

*Bird, Caroline, *Born female: the high cost of keeping women down*, McKay, 1968.

Chombart de Lauwe, M.-J. and P.-H., *La femme dans la société*, Paris, 1963.

Clark, F. Le Gros, *Woman, Work and Age*, London, 1962.

Dahlström, Edmund, *The changing roles of men and women*, London, Stockholm, 1967.

Dodge, Norton T., *Women in the Soviet Economy*, Baltimore, 1966.

Donna (La) nelle societa italiana in trasformazione, ACLI, Rome, 1966.

Douglas, James W. B., The Home and the School, London, 1964.

Dufourcq, Elisabeth, *Les femmes Japonaises*, Paris, 1969.

Franken, Van Driel, P. M., *Europees vrouwenleven*, Amsterdam, 1955.

Friedan, Betty, *The Feminine Mystique*, New York, 1963; *The Feminine Mystique*, London, 1963.

Gerstein, Hannelore, *Studierende Mädchen*, Munich, 1965.

*Gilman, Charlotte Perkins, *Women and Economics*, London; Boston, 1898.

Gössmann, Elisabeth, *Mann und Frau in Familie und Öffentlichkeit*, Munich, 1964.

Gregoire, Ménie, *Le métier de femme*, Paris, 1965.

Gubbels, Robert, *Le travail au féminin*, Bruxelles, 1967.

Guelaud-Leridon, Françoise, *Recherches sur la condition féminine dans la société d'aujourd'hui*, Paris, 1967.

Guilbert, Madeleine, *Les fonctions des femmes dans l'industrie*, Paris, 1966.

Klein, Viola, *Emploi des femmes, horaires et responsabilités*, OECD, 1965.

Klein, Viola, *The Feminine Character: History of an Ideology*, New York, 1946.

Klein, Viola and Myrdal, Alva, *Women's two roles*, London, 1956.

Kok, G. H. S., *Rapport sur la situation politique, sociale, civique de la femme en Europe*, Conseil de l'Europe, Strasbourg, 1967.

Kraditor, Aileen S., *Ideas of the Women's Suffrage Movement, 1890–1920*, Columbia, 1965.

*Michael, Donald, *Cybernation*, Santa Barbara, Center for the Study of Democratic Institutions, 1965.

Michel, A. and Texier, G., *La condition de la Française d'aujourd'hui*, Paris, 1964.

Mitchell, Juliet, 'The Longest Revolution', *New Left Review*, **40**, Nov–Dec 1966.

M'Rabet, Fadéla, *Les Algériennes*, Paris, 1967.

Newcomer, Mabel, *A Century of Higher Education for Women*, New York, 1959.

*O'Neill, William L., 'Feminism as a radical ideology', *Dissent: Explorations in the History of American Radicalism*, Alfred E. Young (ed.), N. Illinois Univ. Press, 1968, pp. 273–300.

*Petersen, William, *The Politics of Population*, New York, 1964.

Pierre, André, *Les femmes en Union Soviétique*, Paris, 1961.

*Pilpel, Harriet, and Zavin, Theodora, *Your Marriage and the Law*, Collier, 1952; revised 1965.

*Rainwater, Lee, Coleman, Richard, P., and Handel, Gerald, *Workingman's wife: Her personality, world and life style*, New York, 1959.

Rotzoll, Christa *et. al.*, *Emanzipation und Ehe*, Munich, 1968.

Sartin, Pierrette, *La promotion des femmes*, Paris, 1964.

Sartin, Pierrette, *La femme libérée?*, Paris, 1969.

Schlesinger, Rudolf (ed.), *Changing Attitudes in Soviet Russia, The Family*, London, 1949.

Sullerot, Evelyne, *La Presse Féminine*, Paris, 1965.

Sullerot, Evelyne, *La Vie des Femmes*, Paris, 1965.

Sullerot, Evelyne, *Demain les Femmes*, Paris, 1966.

Sullerot, Evelyne, *Histoire et Sociologie du Travail féminin*, Paris, 1968.

Wissenlinck, Erika, *Die unfertige Emanzipation; Die Frau in der veränderten Gesellschaft*, Munich, 1965.

Woman (The) in America, Daedalus (special number) Journal of the American Academy of Sciences, New York, 1964.

Women Workers, TUC, London, 1965.

Women Workers, annual handbooks of the Women's Bureau, Department of Labor, Washington.

Publications of the United Nations Commission on the status of women.

International Labor Review (Revue Internationale du Travail), ILO (OIT) Geneva.

Acknowledgments

Tables and figures have been adapted from the following sources:
Tables 2:1 Annuario di statistiche demografiche, vol. XIV, 1964; 2: 3 United Nations Yearbook 1966; 2:4 Statistik arsbok 1967, Stockholm; 2:6 Statistical Yearbook, 1968; 3: 2 US Department of Labor, Current Population Reports, No. 22; 3:4 Institut National d'Etudes Démographiques, Travaux et Documents, No. 42; 3:5 Spanish National Institute of Statistics; 4:1 OECD 1968 (data for Eastern European countries from UN Yearbook 1966); 4:2 Institut National du Statistique et d'Etudes Economiques, 1966; 4:3 Annual Abstract, 1967; 5:1 OIT, Annuaire des statistiques du travail, 1967; 5:2 Ministère des Affaires Sociales, France 1964; 5:3 US Department of Labor – Bureau of Labor Statistics; 5:4 Federal Government Press and Information Service, 1962; 6:3 UNESCO; 6:8 UNESCO, Statistical Yearbook 1966.
Figures 4 Ministry of Labour, France 1963; 5 OECD; 6 US Department of Labor, Bureau of Labor Statistics; 7 Economic Council of Canada; 8 US Department of Commerce, Bureau of the Census; 9 US Department of Health, Education and Welfare, Office of Education.

Acknowledgment is also due to the following for the illustrations (the numbers refer to the page on which the illustration appears):
Frontispiece Chantal Howard, New York; 11, 146, 177 Afrique Photo, Paris; 12, 243 Göksin Sipahioglu, Paris; 16, 37, 103 H.W. Silvester, France; 22–3, 24–5, 81, 92, 136, 137 (top); 145 (top and bottom), 149 Mansell Collection, London; 32, 54, 163, 186 Mary Evans, London; 53, 210 Snark International, Paris; 57, 76, 84, 90, 105, 106, 113, 128, 140, 159, 164, 166, 182, 189, 190, 195, 204, 227, 241 Niépce-Rapho, Paris; 60, 63, 137 (bottom), 203 Radio Times Hulton Picture Library, London; 61, 121 J. Allan Cash, London; 83 (top) Wolf Huber, Diessen; 83 (bottom) Milan Pavić, Zagreb; 104, 150, 171, 220 Novosti Press, London; 116 Fikret Otyam, Ankara; 117, 219 Max Scheler, Hamburg, copyright Stern; 153 Thomas Höpker, Hamburg; 174 Hilman Pabel, Aegidienberg; 196–7 Royal Institution of Great Britain; 224 Central Press Photos, London; 229 Suzanne Szasz, New York; 235 Rudolf Dietrich, Munich; 236 Keystone Press, London; 243 Giancarlo Botti, Photographic Service Monique Valentin, Paris.

The figures were drawn by Design Practitioners Ltd.

Index

Bold figures refer to diagrams or tables

World University Library

Some books published or in preparation

Economics and Social Studies

The World Cities
Peter Hall, *Reading*

The Economics of Underdeveloped Countries
Jagdish Bhagwati, *MIT*

Development Planning
Jan Tinbergen, *Rotterdam*

Human Communication
J. L. Aranguren, *Madrid*

Education in the Modern World
John Vaizey, *London*

Soviet Economics
Michael Kaser, *Oxford*

Decisive Forces in World Economics
J. L. Sampedro, *Madrid*

Key Issues in Criminology
Roger Hood and Richard Sparks, *Cambridge*

Population and History
E. A. Wrigley, *Cambridge*

Woman, Society and Change
Evelyne Sullerot, *Paris*

Power and Society in Africa
Jacques Maquet, *Paris*

History

The Emergence of Greek Democracy
W. G. Forrest, *Oxford*

Muhammad and the Conquests of Islam
Francesco Gabrieli, *Rome*

The Civilisation of Charlemagne
Jacques Boussard, *Poitiers*

Humanism in the Renaissance
S. Dresden, *Leyden*

The Rise of Toleration
Henry Kamen, *Warwick*

Science and Change 1500-1700
Hugh Kearney, *Sussex*

The Left in Europe
David Caute, *London*

The Rise of the Working Class
Jürgen Kuczynski, *Berlin*

Chinese Communism
Robert North, *Stanford*

The Italian City Republics
Daniel Waley, *London*

Rome: The Story of an Empire
J. P. V. D. Balsdon, *Oxford*

Cosmology
Jean Charon

The Arts

Twentieth Century Music
H. H. Stuckenschmidt, *Berlin*

Art Nouveau
S. Tschudi Madsen, *Oslo*

Palaeolithic Cave Art
P. J. Ucko and A. Rosenfeld, *London*

Expressionism
John Willett, *London*

Language and Literature

Two Centuries of French Literature
Raymond Picard, *Paris*

Russian Writers and Society 1825-1904
Ronald Hingley, *Oxford*

Satire
Matthew Hodgart, *Sussex*

255